INTEREST GROUPS
AND ELECTIONS
IN CANADA

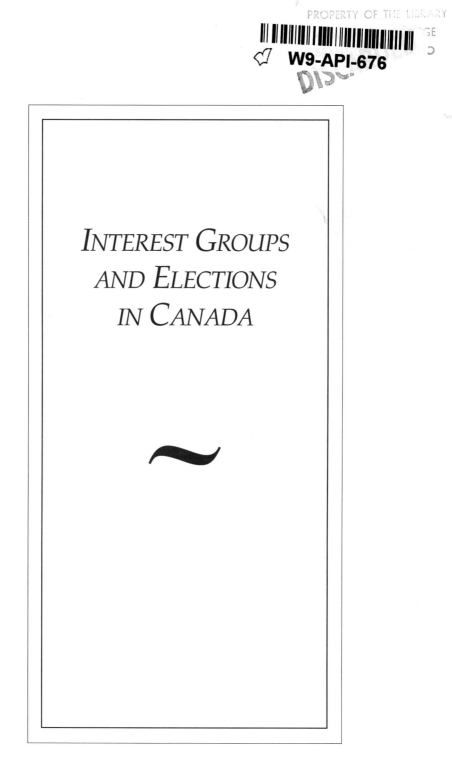

*This is Volume 2 in a series of studies
commissioned as part of the research program
of the Royal Commission on Electoral Reform
and Party Financing*

INTEREST
GROUPS AND
ELECTIONS IN
CANADA

~

F. Leslie Seidle
Editor

Volume 2 of the Research Studies

ROYAL COMMISSION ON ELECTORAL REFORM
AND PARTY FINANCING
AND CANADA COMMUNICATION GROUP –
PUBLISHING, SUPPLY AND SERVICES CANADA

DUNDURN PRESS
TORONTO AND OXFORD

© Minister of Supply and Services Canada, 1991
Printed and bound in Canada
ISBN 1-55002-098-6
ISSN 1188-2743
Catalogue No. Z1-1989/2-41-2E

Published by Dundurn Press Limited in cooperation with the Royal Commission on Electoral Reform and Party Financing and Canada Communication Group – Publishing, Supply and Services Canada.

Canadian Cataloguing in Publication Data

Main entry under title:
Interest groups and elections in Canada

(Research studies ; 2)
Issued also in French under title: Les Groupes d'intérêt et les élections
   au Canada.
ISBN 1-55002-098-6

 1. Pressure groups – Canada. 2. Canada. Parliament – Elections.
I. Seidle, F. Leslie. II. Canada. Royal Commission on Electoral Reform and Party Financing. III. Series: Research studies (Canada. Royal Commission on Electoral Reform and Party Financing) ; 2.

JL193.I58 1991   324'.4'0971   C91-090514-2

$19.95

Dundurn Press Limited
2181 Queen Street East
Suite 301
Toronto, Canada
M4E 1E5

Dundurn Distribution
73 Lime Walk
Headington
Oxford, England
0X3 7AD

CONTENTS

FIGURES

1. INTEREST GROUPS AND CANADIAN FEDERAL ELECTIONS

TABLES

1. INTEREST GROUPS AND CANADIAN FEDERAL ELECTIONS

2. POLITICAL ACTIVITY OF LOCAL INTEREST GROUPS

FOREWORD

THE ROYAL COMMISSION on Electoral Reform and Party Financing
was established in November 1989. Our mandate was to inquire into
and report on the appropriate principles and process that should govern the election of members of the House of Commons and the financing of political parties and candidates' campaigns. To conduct such a
comprehensive examination of Canada's electoral system, we held
extensive public consultations and developed a research program
designed to ensure that our recommendations would be guided by an
independent foundation of empirical inquiry and analysis.

The Commission's in-depth review of the electoral system was the
first of its kind in Canada's history of electoral democracy. It was dictated largely by the major constitutional, social and technological
changes of the past several decades, which have transformed Canadian
society, and their concomitant influence on Canadians' expectations
of the political process itself. In particular, the adoption in 1982 of the
Canadian Charter of Rights and Freedoms has heightened Canadians'
awareness of their democratic and political rights and of the way they
are served by the electoral system.

The importance of electoral reform cannot be overemphasized. As
the Commission's work proceeded, Canadians became increasingly
preoccupied with constitutional issues that have the potential to change
the nature of Confederation. No matter what their beliefs or political
allegiances in this continuing debate, Canadians agree that constitutional
change must be achieved in the context of fair and democratic processes. We cannot complacently assume that our current electoral
process will always meet this standard or that it leaves no room for
improvement. Parliament and the national government must be seen
as legitimate; electoral reform can both enhance the stature of national

political institutions and reinforce their ability to define the future of our country in ways that command Canadians' respect and confidence and promote the national interest.

In carrying out our mandate, we remained mindful of the importance of protecting our democratic heritage, while at the same time balancing it against the emerging values that are injecting a new dynamic into the electoral system. If our system is to reflect the realities of Canadian political life, then reform requires more than mere tinkering with electoral laws and practices.

Our broad mandate challenged us to explore a full range of options. We commissioned more than 100 research studies, to be published in a 23-volume collection. In the belief that our electoral laws must measure up to the very best contemporary practice, we examined election-related laws and processes in all of our provinces and territories and studied comparable legislation and processes in established democracies around the world. This unprecedented array of empirical study and expert opinion made a vital contribution to our deliberations. We made every effort to ensure that the research was both intellectually rigorous and of practical value. All studies were subjected to peer review, and many of the authors discussed their preliminary findings with members of the political and academic communities at national symposiums on major aspects of the electoral system.

The Commission placed the research program under the able and inspired direction of Dr. Peter Aucoin, Professor of Political Science and Public Administration at Dalhousie University. We are confident that the efforts of Dr. Aucoin, together with those of the research coordinators and scholars whose work appears in this and other volumes, will continue to be of value to historians, political scientists, parliamentarians and policy makers, as well as to thoughtful Canadians and the international community.

Along with the other Commissioners, I extend my sincere gratitude to the entire Commission staff for their dedication and commitment. I also wish to thank the many people who participated in our symposiums for their valuable contributions, as well as the members of the research and practitioners' advisory groups whose counsel significantly aided our undertaking.

Pierre Lortie
Chairman

INTRODUCTION

THE ROYAL COMMISSION's research program constituted a comprehensive and detailed examination of the Canadian electoral process. The scope of the research, undertaken to assist Commissioners in their deliberations, was dictated by the broad mandate given to the Commission.

The objective of the research program was to provide Commissioners with a full account of the factors that have shaped our electoral democracy. This dictated, first and foremost, a focus on federal electoral law, but our inquiries also extended to the Canadian constitution, including the institutions of parliamentary government, the practices of political parties, the mass media and nonpartisan political organizations, as well as the decision-making role of the courts with respect to the constitutional rights of citizens. Throughout, our research sought to introduce a historical perspective in order to place the contemporary experience within the Canadian political tradition.

We recognized that neither our consideration of the factors shaping Canadian electoral democracy nor our assessment of reform proposals would be as complete as necessary if we failed to examine the experiences of Canadian provinces and territories and of other democracies. Our research program thus emphasized comparative dimensions in relation to the major subjects of inquiry.

Our research program involved, in addition to the work of the Commission's research coordinators, analysts and support staff, over 200 specialists from 28 universities in Canada, from the private sector and, in a number of cases, from abroad. Specialists in political science constituted the majority of our researchers, but specialists in law, economics, management, computer sciences, ethics, sociology and communications, among other disciplines, were also involved.

In addition to the preparation of research studies for the Commission, our research program included a series of research seminars, symposiums and workshops. These meetings brought together the Commissioners, researchers, representatives from the political parties, media personnel and others with practical experience in political parties, electoral politics and public affairs. These meetings provided not only a forum for discussion of the various subjects of the Commission's mandate, but also an opportunity for our research to be assessed by those with an intimate knowledge of the world of political practice.

These public reviews of our research were complemented by internal and external assessments of each research report by persons qualified in the area; such assessments were completed prior to our decision to publish any study in the series of research volumes.

The Research Branch of the Commission was divided into several areas, with the individual research projects in each area assigned to the research coordinators as follows:

F. Leslie Seidle	Political Party and Election Finance
Herman Bakvis	Political Parties
Kathy Megyery	Women, Ethno-Cultural Groups and Youth
David Small	Redistribution; Electoral Boundaries; Voter Registration
Janet Hiebert	Party Ethics
Michael Cassidy	Democratic Rights; Election Administration
Robert A. Milen	Aboriginal Electoral Participation and Representation
Frederick J. Fletcher	Mass Media and Broadcasting in Elections
David Mac Donald (Assistant Research Coordinator)	Direct Democracy

These coordinators identified appropriate specialists to undertake research, managed the projects and prepared them for publication. They also organized the seminars, symposiums and workshops in their research areas and were responsible for preparing presentations and briefings to help the Commission in its deliberations and decision making. Finally, they participated in drafting the Final Report of the Commission.

On behalf of the Commission, I welcome the opportunity to thank the following for their generous assistance in producing these research studies – a project that required the talents of many individuals.

In performing their duties, the research coordinators made a notable contribution to the work of the Commission. Despite the pressures of tight deadlines, they worked with unfailing good humour and the utmost congeniality. I thank all of them for their consistent support and cooperation.

In particular, I wish to express my gratitude to Leslie Seidle, senior research coordinator, who supervised our research analysts and support staff in Ottawa. His diligence, commitment and professionalism not only set high standards, but also proved contagious. I am grateful to Kathy Megyery, who performed a similar function in Montreal with equal aplomb and skill. Her enthusiasm and dedication inspired us all.

On behalf of the research coordinators and myself, I wish to thank our research analysts: Daniel Arsenault, Eric Bertram, Cécile Boucher, Peter Constantinou, Yves Denoncourt, David Docherty, Luc Dumont, Jane Dunlop, Scott Evans, Véronique Garneau, Keith Heintzman, Paul Holmes, Hugh Mellon, Cheryl D. Mitchell, Donald Padget, Alain Pelletier, Dominique Tremblay and Lisa Young. The Research Branch was strengthened by their ability to carry out research in a wide variety of areas, their intellectual curiosity and their team spirit.

The work of the research coordinators and analysts was greatly facilitated by the professional skills and invaluable cooperation of Research Branch staff members: Paulette LeBlanc, who, as administrative assistant, managed the flow of research projects; Hélène Leroux, secretary to the research coordinators, who produced briefing material for the Commissioners and who, with Lori Nazar, assumed responsibility for monitoring the progress of research projects in the latter stages of our work; Kathleen McBride and her assistant Natalie Brose, who created and maintained the database of briefs and hearings transcripts; and Richard Herold and his assistant Susan Dancause, who were responsible for our research library. Jacinthe Séguin and Cathy Tucker also deserve thanks – in addition to their duties as receptionists, they assisted in a variety of ways to help us meet deadlines.

We were extremely fortunate to obtain the research services of first-class specialists from the academic and private sectors. Their contributions are found in this and the other 22 published research volumes. We thank them for the quality of their work and for their willingness to contribute and to meet our tight deadlines.

Our research program also benefited from the counsel of Jean-Marc Hamel, Special Adviser to the Chairman of the Commission and former

Chief Electoral Officer of Canada, whose knowledge and experience proved invaluable.

In addition, numerous specialists assessed our research studies. Their assessments not only improved the quality of our published studies, but also provided us with much-needed advice on many issues. In particular, we wish to single out professors Donald Blake, Janine Brodie, Alan Cairns, Kenneth Carty, John Courtney, Peter Desbarats, Jane Jenson, Richard Johnston, Vincent Lemieux, Terry Morley and Joseph Wearing, as well as Ms. Beth Symes.

Producing such a large number of studies in less than a year requires a mastery of the skills and logistics of publishing. We were fortunate to be able to count on the Commission's Director of Communications, Richard Rochefort, and Assistant Director, Hélène Papineau. They were ably supported by the Communications staff: Patricia Burden, Louise Dagenais, Caroline Field, Claudine Labelle, France Langlois, Lorraine Maheux, Ruth McVeigh, Chantal Morissette, Sylvie Patry, Jacques Poitras and Claudette Rouleau-O'Toole.

To bring the project to fruition, the Commission also called on specialized contractors. We are deeply grateful for the services of Ann McCoomb (references and fact checking); Marthe Lemery, Pierre Chagnon and the staff of Communications Com'ça (French quality control); Norman Bloom, Pamela Riseborough and associates of B&B Editorial Consulting (English adaptation and quality control); and Mado Reid (French production). Al Albania and his staff at Acart Graphics designed the studies and produced some 2 400 tables and figures.

The Commission's research reports constitute Canada's largest publishing project of 1991. Successful completion of the project required close cooperation between the public and private sectors. In the public sector, we especially acknowledge the excellent service of the Privy Council unit of the Translation Bureau, Department of the Secretary of State of Canada, under the direction of Michel Parent, and our contacts Ruth Steele and Terry Denovan of the Canada Communication Group, Department of Supply and Services.

The Commission's co-publisher for the research studies was Dundurn Press of Toronto, whose exceptional service is gratefully acknowledged. Wilson & Lafleur of Montreal, working with the Centre de Documentation Juridique du Québec, did equally admirable work in preparing the French version of the studies.

Teams of editors, copy editors and proofreaders worked diligently under stringent deadlines with the Commission and the publishers to prepare some 20 000 pages of manuscript for design, typesetting and printing. The work of these individuals, whose names are listed elsewhere in this volume, was greatly appreciated.

Our acknowledgements extend to the contributions of the Commission's Executive Director, Guy Goulard, and the administration and executive support teams: Maurice Lacasse, Denis Lafrance and Steve Tremblay (finance); Thérèse Lacasse and Mary Guy-Shea (personnel); Cécile Desforges (assistant to the Executive Director); Marie Dionne (administration); Anna Bevilacqua (records); and support staff members Michelle Bélanger, Roch Langlois, Michel Lauzon, Jean Mathieu, David McKay and Pierrette McMurtie, as well as Denise Miquelon and Christiane Séguin of the Montreal office.

A special debt of gratitude is owed to Marlène Girard, assistant to the Chairman. Her ability to supervise the logistics of the Commission's work amid the tight schedules of the Chairman and Commissioners contributed greatly to the completion of our task.

I also wish to express my deep gratitude to my own secretary, Liette Simard. Her superb administrative skills and great patience brought much-appreciated order to my penchant for the chaotic workstyle of academe. She also assumed responsibility for the administrative coordination of revisions to the final drafts of volumes 1 and 2 of the Commission's Final Report. I owe much to her efforts and assistance.

Finally, on behalf of the research coordinators and myself, I wish to thank the Chairman, Pierre Lortie, the members of the Commission, Pierre Fortier, Robert Gabor, William Knight and Lucie Pépin, and former members Elwood Cowley and Senator Donald Oliver. We are honoured to have worked with such an eminent and thoughtful group of Canadians, and we have benefited immensely from their knowledge and experience. In particular, we wish to acknowledge the creativity, intellectual rigour and energy our Chairman brought to our task. His unparalleled capacity to challenge, to bring out the best in us, was indeed inspiring.

Peter Aucoin
Director of Research

PREFACE

Twenty-five years ago, following a review of the costs of election campaigns, the pattern of party finance and related issues, the Committee on Election Expenses (Barbeau Committee) issued its report. The Committee's conclusions provided the basis for the 1974 *Election Expenses Act*, which led to what was then considered Canada's most comprehensive regulatory framework for party and election finance. The main elements of the 1974 reforms were: limits on the election expenses of registered political parties and candidates; disclosure of parties' and candidates' revenue and spending; and public funding through post-election reimbursements to parties and candidates, as well as an income tax credit for contributions to either.

While amendments in 1977 and 1983 did not alter the main lines of the federal regulatory framework, developments during the past 15 years or so have led to calls for an assessment of its operation and effects. Some have asked whether the objectives on which the 1974 legislation was based are still being met – or, indeed, remain valid. A number of factors account for this, among them changes in party and campaign management techniques, the implications of the adoption of the *Canadian Charter of Rights and Freedoms* in 1982, the role of interest groups in elections and developments in the regulation of political finance at the provincial level.

The Royal Commission on Electoral Reform and Party Financing was mandated to consider, among other issues, "the appropriate principles and process that should govern ... the financing of political parties and of candidates' campaigns, including ... the means by which political parties should be funded, the provision of funds to political parties from any source, the limits on such funding and the uses to which such funds ought, or ought not, to be put." To assist it in carrying out these aspects of its mandate, an extensive series of research studies on party and election finance was undertaken by members of the academic profession, consultants and research analysts employed by the Commission. The principal studies are published in this volume and the four others in this research area.

The research projects in the party and election finance area were intended to assist the Commission in taking decisions on a number of issues at the heart of its mandate. In this regard, the studies in these five volumes are relevant to three of the six objectives of electoral reform referred to in Volume 1, chapter 1 of the Final Report: promoting fairness in the electoral process; strengthening the parties as primary political organizations; and enhancing public confidence in the integrity of the electoral process. These studies canvass issues relevant to these objectives, draw on comparative experience (both within Canada and elsewhere) and discuss possible reforms. In so doing, they address fundamental questions such as: how to circumscribe the influence of money in politics; how to encourage greater participation in the financing of parties and candidates and in the electoral process, including the nomination stage; how to ensure a high degree of transparency in relation to political finance; and whether and in what ways public funding should be part of the system.

The studies in this volume address one of the most fundamental questions the Commission faced: whether and how to regulate spending during elections by persons and groups other than candidates and registered political parties – the spending referred to as "independent expenditures" in Volume 1 of the Final Report. This question figured prominently in the Commission's hearings, and many interveners, recalling the debate on free trade during the 1988 election, stressed that the approach to independent expenditures would have to be determined in relation to the federal regulatory framework as a whole, particularly the election spending limits.

Janet Hiebert's study, "Interest Groups and Canadian Federal Elections," reviews interest group activity, including costs incurred, at the national level during the 1988 election. An opening had been provided by the 1984 Alberta court decision that struck down the 1983 legislative ban on independent expenditures, except in relation to issues, and by the subsequent lack of enforcement of the existing law elsewhere in the country. Dr. Hiebert suggests there is now an asymmetry between the absence of effective restrictions on interest group election expenses and the spending limits for candidates and political parties. In assessing reform options, she underlines the importance of the principles of equity and fairness, which she refers to as the cornerstones of the Canadian federal election process, and suggests that the reasonableness of limits on independent expenditures would be determined by the degree to which, in seeking to respect these principles, freedom of speech is affected.

In their research study, "Political Activity of Local Interest Groups," Brian Tanguay and Barry Kay report the findings of their survey of 89 locally oriented interest groups. The authors include a case study of the candidate-directed activities of Campaign Life, an anti-abortion group, during the 1988 election. On the question of the desirability of independent expenditures, they found the interest groups were about evenly split, with a slight majority in favour of such activity not being allowed. They also found that the groups most critical of the status quo (labour groups, moral/ethical groups and environmental organizations) were consistently in favour of relatively unrestricted independent expenditures, while the groups most satisfied with the political system (business groups and those representing the social service sector) were most opposed.

The Commission owes a considerable debt of gratitude to the researchers who agreed to undertake the studies in this area. Through their dedication and professionalism, their responsiveness to the Commission's priorities and their cooperation in meeting deadlines, all those whose work appears in these volumes have contributed greatly to the research program. A number of the researchers presented their findings at Commission seminars and/or meetings. We valued their participation on these occasions, as well as their willingness to respond to a range of questions and requests for information, particularly during the period when the Commission's Final Report was being prepared. I would also like to express my personal gratitude to Peter Aucoin, whose suggestions and counsel helped in so many ways as these research studies were planned, discussed and carried forward for publication.

The Commission's publication program reflects the central role research played in the work of the Royal Commission on Electoral Reform and Party Financing. It is hoped these studies will illuminate debate on the Commission's recommendations and, in so doing, help chart the way to a modern and responsive regulatory framework for party and election finance that will bolster electoral democracy in Canada.

F. Leslie Seidle
Senior Research Coordinator

INTEREST GROUPS AND ELECTIONS IN CANADA

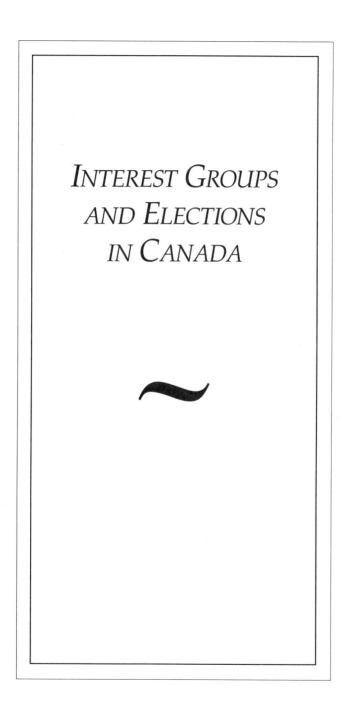

1

INTEREST GROUPS AND CANADIAN FEDERAL ELECTIONS

Janet Hiebert

POLITICAL PARTIES HAVE long assumed the lead position on the Canadian electoral stage. Unlike candidate-centred elections in the United States, where parties are a distant second to the candidates themselves (and even lag behind special interest groups in their ability to raise and direct money for elections), the primacy of parties in Canadian elections has traditionally gone unchallenged. This primacy has reflected the central role that parties play in providing a vehicle for Canadians' preferences to be interpreted and ordered by government. The capacity of the three larger national parties to represent the multitude of interests in Canadian society is, however, increasingly being questioned. The fragmentation of election discourse as a result of an increasing role by interest groups is indication that parties' proprietary claim on the election stage is the subject of debate.

This debate will be explored in this study in terms of the nexus during elections between interest groups, and parties and candidates. Increased election involvement by interest groups, most notably in the 1988 general election, has introduced a new dynamic to election contests and has raised questions about the fairness and efficacy of the existing regulatory regime.

Equity and fairness are the cornerstones of the Canadian election regulatory regime. Commitment to equity underlies the regulations governing the amount that candidates and parties can spend to contest federal elections, and these regulations are enforced by the requirement of disclosure. The rationale for such regulations is to address problems that can arise from the role of money in elections: money which, if unregulated, can distort campaigns by allowing concentrated wealth to "drown" the voices of individuals, alter the agenda, and create perceptions that elections can be "bought." Equity in resources among candidates is not the only objective, although this may prevent cynicism in the electoral process. The measures promote fairness by establishing a low economic threshold for those seeking election participation and by allowing for reimbursement to ensure that the requirements for seeking office do not discriminate against persons of modest means. Furthermore, broadcasting regulations governing when and how candidates and parties can advertise, together with the equitable treatment of spending limits, foster fairness by ensuring that candidates seeking election cannot rely on private wealth or special interest funds to gain economic advantages over partisan rivals. These spending limits establish what is widely referred to as a "level playing field."

Concomitant with these attempts to ensure that money does not unduly distort the election process or unfairly disadvantage those of modest means who seek office have been regulations governing the financial activities of other election participants, including interest groups, corporations and unions, generically referred to as "third parties."[1] Regulations dating back to 1974 have sought to ensure that nonregistered participants cannot spend money in ways that would undermine the principles of equity and fairness or would nullify the significance of candidate and party finance laws and broadcast regulations.

Constitutional developments and policy decisions affecting the enforcement of regulations for interest groups, however, have produced a situation in which individuals or groups (other than registered candidates and parties) are operating in an essentially unregulated election environment. In contrast, the spending and broadcast regulations governing candidates and parties remain intact. This asymmetry in the regulatory framework not only raises questions of whether the principles of equity and fairness among candidates are endangered, but also reveals the need to rethink the entire approach to regulating election expenditures.

In considering the appropriate nexus during federal elections between interest groups and parties/candidates, this study will analyse institutional factors that influence the electoral process (such as the role of parties and constitutional imperatives), arguments for and against greater interest group participation, and the 1988 federal and 1990 Ontario provincial elections where there were significant interest group expenditures independent of registered candidates and parties. The study will also examine comparative experiences in other provinces as well as in Britain, France and the United States to consider what lessons can be learned from the regulatory approaches of other regimes. The purpose of the study is to explore regulatory options for Canada.

INSTITUTIONAL FRAMEWORK

Before examining the question of what role interest groups should play in federal elections, two institutional factors should be considered: the role of political parties and the constitutional context in which all legislation must be assessed. The reason that these factors should be addressed, if only briefly, is because they affect directly the kind of political and electoral process that government wishes to promote.

Political Parties

It is generally accepted that parties are expected to serve "as a bridge between state actions and the interests and demands of society" (Jenson 1991). Political parties are fundamental to the operation of government in our parliamentary democracy. Parties are expected to represent the varied and diverse interests of Canadian society and to provide the vehicle by which this multiplicity of values is reconciled and ordered in the choosing of a government.

> In our age of universal adult suffrage Responsible Government has developed into a system of government by cohesive political parties largely to prevent the House from acting as a congress or as a ministerial electoral college. Under party government each party selects its leader and its key players. It acquires its own style, character, and complexion. These are set before the voters at each election. By means of political parties with known leaders the electors are given a choice between (or among) potential prime ministers and ministerial teams, and by party cohesion they are assured that their members in the House of Commons will not frustrate their intentions after the election. The people commit the conduct of the government to the ministerial team of a party, and to the general policies of that party. (Stewart 1977, 28)

While not provided for in the written Constitution, the political convention of responsible government, which predates the *Constitution Act, 1867,* has encouraged the development of disciplined political parties. Because the government is dependent on the support of a majority in the House of Commons, members usually divide into two positions: those who support the government and those who oppose it. They further divide according to party. It is through parties that elected members represent the electorate. Because the survival of the government requires the support of the House, members generally participate as a cohesive and unified team (hence the practice of party discipline) rather than as a loose association of individual agents with shifting alliances (Stewart 1977, 28).

That parties are expected to play this crucial role is reflected in the institutional advantages conferred upon them as opposed to individuals or interest groups wanting to participate in the electoral process. A comprehensive financial regulatory regime is built around the central premise that parties are the chief participants in elections. As such, established parties are eligible for substantial financial subsidies in seeking elected office and are the recipients of a generous system of tax credits intended to help sustain them between elections.

Constitutional Framework

The second institutional arrangement that must be considered in determining the appropriate nexus between parties and interest groups during elections is the constitutional framework in which the electoral process operates. The single-member plurality electoral system is an important element that influences the way parties compete in elections and greatly affects the way Canadian votes are translated into representation.[2]

Of more significance in the context of interest group election involvement, however, is the *Canadian Charter of Rights and Freedoms*. Before 1982 the policy process was not structured by consideration of formal rights. The principal constitutional imperative was to ensure that legislation accurately reflected the jurisdictional division of powers as provided in the *Constitution Act, 1867*. The *Canadian Charter of Rights and Freedoms* has changed this.

The notion of entrenched rights is for some a deceptively simple idea. The benefits of entrenchment are widely believed to stem from the regulating impact on governments. Because the Charter imposes standards against which legislation can be evaluated and provides the mandate for courts to declare unconstitutional any legislative or executive act which departs from those standards, many believe that entrenchment provides the ultimate challenge to the long-standing principle of "parliamentary supremacy." This implies, however, that the rights described in the Charter are stated in such a way that courts will readily identify when in fact legislation encroaches upon them. Furthermore, it wrongly assumes that rights are absolute in nature. Preceding the enumerated rights is a general limitation clause, section 1, which explicitly allows for the protected rights to be limited. Section 1 subjects the rights in the Charter to "such reasonable limits, prescribed by law as can be demonstrably justified in a free and democratic society."

Some Charter commentators do not anticipate courts having difficulty recognizing when limits on protected rights are justified. They suggest that while rights can never be absolute, governments should not be allowed to infringe upon them unless they can demonstrate that the disputed policy would facilitate democracy or is necessary because of an emergency (Weinrib 1988, 483). The problem with this approach is that it does not anticipate that interpretations of the scope of protected rights or review of section 1 arguments will turn on competing definitions of what is essential to a democratic system. It is politically naïve to believe that judges will agree about what a free and democratic society entails and will readily identify what is required to facilitate democracy. For example, while it would be difficult to argue that a fair electoral process is not an integral part of a free and democratic society, many disagree over what a fair electoral process encompasses. Furthermore, in the case of reconciling a fair electoral process with freedom of expression, it is not clear from the wording of the Charter which value should be given priority or what weight might be assigned to each value.

Many commentators, including a significant number of those who participated in this Royal Commission's hearings, give insufficient consideration to the role of the limitation clause in section 1 when assuming that interest groups or individuals cannot be regulated because of the presence of freedom of expression in section 2(b) of the Charter. Having argued that it is not obvious what kinds of activities can be considered a reasonable limit on expression in light of section 1, it is important to keep in mind the context for imposing limits on expression, the principles these limits serve, and their impact on expression before making assumptions about the extent to which interest groups are constitutionally entitled to advertise policy positions during elections. Furthermore, while the *Canadian Charter of Rights and Freedoms* has had a significant impact on a central principle of the Canadian political system, the supremacy of Parliament and the provincial legislatures, it has not altered the basic political institutions of Canada, of which parties are at front and centre.

Should Parties Share the Electoral Stage?

The institutional privileges conferred upon parties in the Canadian political system are being questioned. Critics argue that the existing system is desirable neither in terms of the kind of representation and civic participation it promotes nor in terms of the importance assigned to freedom of expression in the Charter. Increasingly, interest and minority groups have questioned the ability of the traditional political parties to represent the wide variety of social, cultural and economic interests that exist in Canada.

A related concern of an exclusive role for parties and candidates during elections is that because elections provide the opportunity for most citizens' only form of direct participation in the political process, individuals should not be discouraged from participating in ways other than as candidates. The justification for this claim lies not only in long-standing notions of democracy and citizenship but also in recently formalized claims to free speech. This opportunity to speak freely is held to be of particular importance during elections when the ability to criticize governments and those seeking public office, without reprisal, is critically important to the vitality and health of the electoral process.

Another argument in favour of allowing interest groups to participate financially in elections is that these groups force parties to address issues that they would otherwise be reluctant to place on the political agenda. To achieve national support, parties are required to appeal to a broad range of interests, and are therefore reluctant to speak to divisive issues which, by their nature, undermine the parties' ability to generate consensus. Interest groups are less constrained in this way because they have a narrower basis of support and, through media pressure, can compel parties to assert policy positions on issues that would otherwise be left off the political agenda. The fact that interest groups are vying for opportunities on the electoral stage itself suggests that there is a considerable gap between the role parties are expected to serve and the role they in fact do assume.

The strongest argument against unregulated interest group electoral participation is that their expenses undermine the principles of fairness and equity among registered participants. The presence of unregulated and unaccountable money directly conflicts with these core principles of our electoral process. The opportunity for any candidate to contest elections on an equitable financial basis with rival candidates, regardless of his or her own personal wealth, is a prerequisite for and a minimal requirement of a fair electoral process. Expenditures independent of the amount that candidates and parties can legally spend, particularly those that parallel in a positive or negative way the issues and programs they promote, directly contradict the principles that private wealth or special interest funds should not undermine equity among registered participants. The value of these principles is that they protect the integrity of a process that is inherently combative and competitive.

The equation of free expression with the ability to spend money during an election is at odds with the fundamental principles of fairness and equity that inform the electoral regulatory regime governing candidates and parties. Furthermore, the assumption that the Charter prevents government from imposing limits on expression denies the fact that expression, both before and after the Charter, has always been subject to limits.

While interest groups would be able to attract more attention to the issues they wish to promote if they had unlimited opportunities to spend money during elections, limits on this ability do not prevent expression in the form of communicating ideas to interested listeners (for example, through telephone and door-to-door campaigns, or regularly published newsletters to members). Financial limits curtail the ability during elections to present this information via the media to a larger audience. The tension between the competing values – freedom of expression on the one hand, and equity and fairness on the other – arises primarily when expression is equated exclusively with the right to spend money.

Like most rights-based claims, arguments about the requirements of free expression can be turned on their heads to provide the counter-arguments. While it is said that freedom of expression must be unfettered, particularly during elections, it is necessary to consider that a corollary of freedom of expression is the ability to receive a well-balanced exposition of issues, particularly from those seeking public office. Because discrepancies in wealth directly affect the ability to communicate a message, it cannot be assumed that unregulated advertising generates a complete and balanced argument of the relevant election issues. If freedom of expression means more than the right to spend money, it can be argued that limits on interest groups' expenditures during elections enhance rather than detract from freedom of expression by ensuring that wealthy individuals and groups do not distort the election agenda by monopolizing the media. This argument is supported by the Supreme Court's finding that free expression, at least in the commercial context, protects the listener as well as the speaker: "Over and above its intrinsic value as expression, commercial expression which, as has been pointed out, protects listeners as well as speakers, plays a significant role in enabling individuals to make informed economic choices, an important aspect of individual self-fulfillment and personal autonomy" (*Ford* 1988, 767).

While the Court was discussing expression from a commercial perspective, an important part of its interpretation was that speech plays a significant role in enabling individuals to make informed economic choices. Such choices are a significant aspect of individual self-fulfilment and personal autonomy. This rationale is even more relevant in the context of election choices where informed voting is the primary and core political activity of most individuals.

However, the argument that freedom of expression is not absolute and must be assessed within the institutional and constitutional context of the Canadian political and electoral system does not presume that parties have exclusive rights to occupy the electoral stage or that interest groups cannot or should not contribute to the electoral process. There is persuasion in the argument that interest group participation can enhance the electoral process by providing an alternative to the existing parties. Furthermore, to the extent that interest groups are not beholden to any one particular party, these groups can serve the important function, otherwise entrusted exclusively to the media, of monitoring and criticizing inconsistencies in party or candidate policy positions and their failure to address important, philosophically divisive issues. Such ideas have even more currency in light of the entrenchment of freedom of expression in the Charter.

The Supreme Court has given strong indication that it considers freedom of expression to be one of the most important democratic values. For instance, in *Ford*, one of the most anxiously awaited Supreme Court decisions, the Court, in an unanimous judgement, found the unilingual business signs provision in the *Charter of the French Language* in conflict with the constitutional guarantee of freedom of expression. The legislation required that public signs, commercial advertising, and names of firms be in French only. In finding that commercial expression was a fundamental right, indeed one of "intrinsic value," the Court interpreted freedom of expression in an extremely broad manner, rejecting the argument that free speech should not be extended to corporate organizations (*Ford* 1988, 767).

In *Irwin Toy Ltd. v. Quebec (Attorney General)*, a subsequent judgement involving free speech, the Court expanded on its earlier finding that commercial advertising is a protected activity by holding that any activity which conveys or attempts to convey meaning has expressive content[3] and prima facie falls within the scope of the guarantee (*Irwin Toy* 1989, 927). Although the majority of the Court upheld the limit on speech under section 1, Justice William McIntyre, in dissent, advanced an extremely broad interpretation to freedom of expression, and suggested that the Court should not uphold limits on it except for urgent and compelling reasons: "Freedom of expression, whether political, religious, artistic or commercial, should not be suppressed except in cases where urgent and compelling reasons exist and then only to the extent and for the time necessary for the protection of the community" (ibid., 1009).

The Court further developed its approach to freedom of expression in *R. v. Keegstra* when it held in a 4–3 decision that free speech in section 2(*b*) of the Charter protects all forms of expression, including communications that wilfully promote hatred against an identifiable group. Writing for the majority, Brian Dickson, then Chief Justice, suggested that although he was reluctant to limit speech pertaining to political matters, hate propaganda "strays some distance from the spirit of s. 2(*b*)," and, therefore, is easier to justify than other infringements on free speech (*Keegstra* 1990, 187). Nevertheless, despite upholding federal legislation making it illegal to advance hate literature as a reasonable limit, he gave a strong indication that free speech, particularly political expression, is at the heart of democratic values:

> The connection between freedom of expression and the political process is perhaps the linchpin of the s. 2(b) guarantee, and the nature of this connection is largely derived from the Canadian commitment to democracy. Freedom of expression is a crucial aspect of the democratic commitment, not merely because it permits the best policies to be chosen from among a wide array of proffered opinions, but additionally because it helps to ensure that participation in the political process is open to all persons. Such open participation must involve to a substantial degree the notion that all persons are equally deserving of respect and dignity. The state therefore cannot act to hinder or condemn a political view without to some extent harming the openness of Canadian democracy and its associated tenet of equality for all. (ibid., 185)

Dickson's comments suggest that future challenges to limits on individuals' or interest groups' abilities to express themselves during elections may receive considerable judicial sympathy. While entrenchment does not mean that the principles of fairness and equity are no longer valid constitutional objectives, it does mean that the pursuit of these values will require that the government demonstrably justify any limits to affected rights – in this case freedom of expression.

The question that must be asked, therefore, is not whether interest group activity should be encouraged or discouraged, but: given the central role parties play in the election process, to what extent can interest groups financially participate in elections without significantly and irreparably undermining the fundamental principles of the system by which we exercise self-rule, choose our government and order our preferences?

HISTORICAL LIMITS ON INTEREST GROUPS

As early as 1966 when partial spending limits for candidates were proposed by the Barbeau Committee,[4] the recognition came that these limits would be meaningful only if accompanied by regulations on the
activities of other electoral participants. To address the possibility that
interest groups could undermine expenditure limits for candidates, the
Committee recommended that all groups other than registered parties
and nominated candidates be prevented from using paid advertisements that directly promote or oppose a candidate or party during
the election.

> The Committee has no desire to stifle the actions of such groups in
> their day-to-day activities. However, the Committee has learned from
> other jurisdictions that if these groups are allowed to participate
> actively in an election campaign any limitations or controls on the
> political parties or candidates become meaningless. In the United
> States, for example, ad hoc committees such as "friends of John Smith"
> or "Supporters of John Doe" commonly spring up to support a can-
> didate or party. Such committees make limitation on expenditures an
> exercise in futility, and render meaningless the reporting of election
> expenses by parties and candidates. (Canada, Committee 1966, 50)

In making the recommendation that interest group advertising be prohibited during elections, the Committee recognized that these restrictions "may encroach to some extent on their freedom of action" but
justified its decision on the basis that, without such restrictions, any
efforts to limit and control election expenditures would be meaningless. The formal recommendation was that "no groups or bodies other
than registered parties and nominated candidates be permitted to purchase radio and television time, or to use paid advertising in newspapers, periodicals, or direct mailing, posters or billboards, in support
of, or opposition to, any party or candidate, from the date of the issuance
of the election writ until the day after polling day" (Canada, Committee
1966, 50).

The Barbeau Committee's recommendations were generally ignored
until a number of factors combined in the early 1970s to encourage
renewed public discussion of party finances and election spending (Seidle
and Paltiel 1981, 231). In 1971 a Special Committee on Election Expenses
was set up by the House of Commons (known as the Chappell
Committee). In its report the Committee recommended a number of
amendments to the *Canada Elections Act* similar to many of those

recommendations found in the Barbeau Report. Consistent with the Barbeau Committee's concern of lowering the cost of federal elections, the Chappell Committee recommended that limits on election expenses be established for both candidates and parties (Canada, House of Commons 1971, 13:21). Like the Barbeau Committee, the Chappell Committee premised the effectiveness of candidate and party limits on the assumption that interest groups be barred from electoral participation. Where it differed, however, was in its prohibition of indirect as well as direct expenditures by interest groups. The recommendation was:

(a) We recommend that, during an election, all election expenses must be authorized by the appropriate official agent of a candidate or of a registered party ...

(c) We recommend that any person, corporation, association or registered party which directly or indirectly incurs election expenses or makes such expenditures, or which between elections incurs any expenses or makes such expenditure on behalf of any registered party, without authorization by the appropriate official agent, be guilty of an offence against the Act.

(d) We recommend that any candidate or any official agent of a candidate or of a registered party who authorizes election expenses otherwise than as permitted by the Act, be guilty of an offence against the Act and of a corrupt practice. (Canada, House of Commons 1971, 13:19)

Legislation enacted in 1974 prohibited interest groups from incurring expenses to promote or oppose candidates or parties. Individuals were deemed to have incurred election expenses if, during the election period, they used broadcasting facilities, procured or acquiesced in the publication of an advertisement in a periodical publication, or distributed any advertising material for the purpose of promoting or opposing a registered party or candidate (*Canada Elections Act*, s. 70.1(3)). Like the Barbeau Report, the legislation reflected concern that the restrictions would have a negative impact on individual expression. In an attempt to minimize the impact of the regulations on interest groups' abilities to participate in elections, the legislation contained an important defence to prosecution. It allowed interest groups to incur expenses to promote or oppose a registered party or candidate if it could be established that the expenditures were incurred in good faith for the purpose of gaining support for the individual's views on an issue of public policy or for advancing the aims of a nonpartisan organization. The "good faith" defence was contained in the following:

70.1(4) Notwithstanding anything in this section, it is a defence to any prosecution of a person for an offence against this Act ... if that person establishes that he incurred election expenses ...

(a) for the purpose of gaining support for views held by him on an issue of public policy, or for the purpose of advancing the aims of any organization or association, other than a political party or an organization or association of a partisan political character, of which he was a member and on whose behalf the expenses were incurred; and

(b) in good faith and not for any purpose related to the provisions of this Act limiting the amount of election expenses that may be incurred by any other person on account of or in respect of the conduct or management of an election.

It soon became apparent that enforcing the good faith defence was problematic and, consequently, the provision had the potential to negate the significance of regulating interest group expenditures. The problems with enforcing the defence arose after an individual was acquitted of violating the law despite an absence of any articulated policy position. The incident involved expenses incurred by Donald Roach, president of a local branch of the Ontario Housing Corporation employees' union. At the request of his local branch, Roach hired an aircraft on the eve of a 1976 by-election in the Ottawa–Carleton riding to tow a banner with the following message: "O.H.C. Employees 767 C.U.P.E. vote but not Liberal." In arguing that the incident contravened the provisions for interest group electoral participation, the government claimed that the statement was not on an issue of public policy or for the advancement of the aims of a nonpartisan political association. The presiding judge disagreed and held that the message was a legitimate attempt to oppose the government's anti-inflation program and to attract publicity which might assist in obtaining further opportunities to advance the policy of C.U.P.E. Local 767, rather than an action to "insert itself in the by-election in a partisan political manner" (*Roach* 1977).

Roach's acquittal raised the question of whether the "good faith" defence could adequately distinguish the promotion of policy issues from the advocacy of candidates and parties. The specific question raised by the decision was whether it was necessary that the advertising message itself refer to an issue of public policy or if the individual or organization sponsoring the message could generate a policy issue after the fact. The matter was no clearer upon appeal. The Appeal Court judge not only found that Roach did not incur election expenses "for the purpose of promoting or opposing directly a registered party or candidate" but that the government had failed to demonstrate that Roach was not expressing the views of his association on an issue of public policy (*Roach* 1978).

Roach's acquittal also contributed to a growing uncertainty about what kind of election activities were allowed under the good faith defence. Elections officials received a large number of requests from individuals wanting an interpretation of the Act. Furthermore, in his Statutory Report of 1979, Chief Electoral Officer Jean-Marc Hamel reported numerous incidents in which individuals had availed themselves of the good faith defence. A result of this defence, in Hamel's view, was that the credibility of the expenditure restrictions for candidates and parties was adversely affected.

> Candidates and political parties are restricted by the Act both in the period when they can advertise in the print and electronic media and in the amounts of money they can spend for the purpose of promoting their election. The legislation imposes no such restrictions on persons, organizations and associations providing they are bona fide and are acting in good faith. The situation seems anomalous and, if permitted to continue, could weaken considerably efforts to control election expenses. Therefore, this is a part of the legislation which Parliament may have to examine. (Canada, Elections Canada 1979, 26)

Hamel restated his concerns in his 1980 Statutory Report, concluding that the good faith defence made it difficult to enforce the intent of the legislation because it was "practically impossible to prove lack of good faith or collusion on the part of individuals or groups who have incurred such expenses" (Canada, Elections Canada 1980, 22). Three years later Hamel proposed in his Statutory Report that the good faith defence be removed and that individuals or interest groups be prevented from incurring expenses to directly oppose or promote a candidate or party.

> As it now stands, the wording of this section permits any person or non-political organization … to directly promote or oppose a particular registered party or the election of a particular candidate. In defending any prosecution initiated under this section, these individuals or organizations may claim that they were "promoting an issue of public policy" or that they were "advancing the aims of their organization" even though they did not identify those issues and/or aims in their advertisements, provided they are able to show they were acting in

good faith ... These people have spent unlimited sums of money to promote or oppose a particular candidate or registered party, sums which they do not have to account for in terms of sources or amount. (Canada, Elections Canada 1983, 74)

The legislation was amended in 1983 in response to Hamel's concerns that the good faith defence undermined the effectiveness of the spending limits. The amended Act effectively prohibited all opportunity for interest groups or individuals to financially oppose candidates or parties during elections and it allowed for the financial promotion of them only when authorized. The amendment provided that anyone other than candidates or official agents who incurred election expenses was guilty of violating the Act:

70.1(1) Every one, other than
  (a) a candidate, official agent or any other person acting on behalf of a candidate with the candidate's actual knowledge and consent,
      or
  (b) a registered agent of a registered party acting within the scope of his authority as such or other person acting on behalf of a registered party with the actual knowledge and consent of an officer thereof,
who, between the date of the issue of the writ for an election and the day immediately following polling day, incurs election expenses is guilty of an offence against this Act.

Election expenses are defined as costs "for the purpose of promoting or opposing, directly and during an election, a particular registered party, or the election of a particular candidate" (*Canada Elections Act*, s. 2(1)). The legislation did not prohibit interest groups from incurring expenses to promote issues as long as the message did not directly identify a party or candidate. In defending the legislation, in fact, the government argued that the provisions do not prevent freedom of expression because they allow interest groups to spend unlimited sums of money to promote issues: "Section 70.1 does not prevent individuals and groups, other than candidates and parties, from exercising freedom of expression ... Individuals and groups ... are still free to spend as much money as they wish during an election to advertise their views on election issues as long as this expenditure of money is not made for the purpose of *directly* promoting or opposing political parties and candidates" (Canada, Attorney General 1984, First Submission, 76–77).

Members from all three parties recognized, in parliamentary debate, that the amendments might conflict with freedom of expression in the Charter but nevertheless justified the repeal of the good faith defence to preserve the values of fairness and equity in elections (Canada, House of Commons 1983, 28295–99).

The legislation was successfully challenged for violating freedom of expression by the National Citizens' Coalition. The decision, which was rendered in the Alberta Queen's Bench, held that the government had not demonstrated the need for the spending regulations for interest groups and that the legislation, therefore, was not justified under section 1 of the Charter. Mr. Justice Donald Medhurst indicated that the legislation could only be justified if the government could demonstrate that mischief or harm would occur without the regulations: "Care must be taken to ensure that the freedom of expression ... is not arbitrarily or unjustifiably limited. Fears or concerns of mischief that may occur are not adequate reasons for imposing a limitation. There should be actual demonstration of harm or a real likelihood of harm to a society value before a limitation can be said to be justified" (*National Citizens' Coalition* 1984, 453).

In finding that the record of mischief caused by interest groups was insufficient,[5] Mr. Justice Medhurst did not disclose why the evidence submitted fell short of the empirical test. The fact that the government's submissions fell short of the requirement that it demonstrate the lesser test of "a real likelihood of harm" leads to the question of whether nothing short of satisfying the more difficult test of "actual demonstration of harm" would have convinced Mr. Justice Medhurst that the limitation was necessary. A serious problem with Mr. Justice Medhurst's empirical test is that it imposed a burden on the government that would have been difficult to meet unless nothing short of blatant corruption had occurred. How else could the government meet Mr. Justice Medhurst's stringent criteria and prove that the failure to impose limits on a Charter right would result in actual demonstration of harm, unless that harm had already occurred?

The inadequacy of Mr. Justice Medhurst's test was not only that it was extremely difficult, if not impossible, to satisfy. A second problem was that he did not address the basic question of whether the limitation on interest groups' financial expression was a valid objective. The spending regulations for interest groups were not assessed in the context of the overall electoral finance regulatory regime, despite urging from the government that they could only be understood by examining the principles of the electoral process: "in assessing the rationality of the limitations on third parties, the Court must assess the rationality of the scheme of regulating election expenses in order to promote equality of electoral opportunity" (Canada, Attorney General 1984, Second Submission, 5).

The decision was rendered before the Supreme Court articulated the criteria for evaluating the reasonableness of legislation found to conflict with a protected right. The Court indicated that only legislation relating to concerns "which are pressing and substantial" in a free and democratic society will be eligible to limit a protected right (*Oakes* 1986, 138–39). In addition to this test, the Court outlined the following objectives:

i) the measures adopted must be rationally connected to the objective and cannot be arbitrary, unfair or based on irrational considerations;

ii) the means should impair "as little as possible" the right or freedom in question; and

iii) there must be a proportionality between the effects of the measure and the objective. (ibid., 139)

While one can only speculate how the Supreme Court might have decided the *National Citizens' Coalition* case in light of these principles, it is clear that the Court does not require "empirical proof of harm" to justify legislation under section 1. The Court, in fact, has asserted that it must be careful "to avoid rigid and inflexible standards" when determining the justification of legislation (*Edwards Books* 1986, 768–69).

It is difficult to predict how the Supreme Court would have decided the *National Citizens' Coalition* case. Nevertheless, a number of observations can be made. The legislative objective of ensuring a fair and equitable electoral process would certainly pass the first test. The Court rarely finds an objective unconstitutional, which is not surprising, given that governments usually enact legislation for valid purposes. Difficulties the government might incur in defending the legislation under section 1 would arise in the second part of the inquiry: did the legislation impair freedom of expression as little as possible? This has become an extremely important question for the Court in resolving such claims. Legislation often passes or fails the section 1 test on the ability of government to convince the Court that no less restrictive means were available to pursue the policy objective. In responding to this test, the argument would likely be that nothing short of a prohibition on interest groups' financial ability to oppose candidates and parties would ensure the viability and fairness of the regulations on registered participants' spending.[6]

Moreover, the degree of impairment was a factor in the legislative decision not to impose a system of registration, spending limits on the promotion of issues, disclosure of donations or reporting to which candidates and parties must adhere (Canada, Attorney General 1984, First Submission, 85–86). Despite these arguments that no other measures were available, it is conceivable that the government would be required to demonstrate why less restrictive limits (than the prohibition of interest group advertisements that explicitly link issues to the promotion of candidates or parties) were not used. If this were the case, it might have been difficult for the government to make a convincing argument that even nominal abilities to link issues with the explicit promotion of candidates would undermine the integrity of the spending regulations.

An argument that can be anticipated in any further challenge to this or similar legislation is whether the promotion of issues during elections, without the ability to link them to the relevant positions of candidates or parties, is an unjustified restriction on expression. In order for citizens to have a significant impact on the choosing and assessing of governments, it is necessary to allow for the criticism of those who seek public office. This is particularly important in the context of judging governments during election periods. Attempts to prevent criticism of incumbent politicians or governments are seen by some as efforts to insulate the established parties from the criticism of interest groups that feel so strongly about a particular cause that they are willing to organize and use whatever financial resources are available to them to persuade their fellow citizens to support their point of view.

If the Court were convinced by this argument, the onus would be on the government to demonstrate that there was no way of allowing groups to "name names" (for example, the enforcement difficulties of maintaining effective limits on the amount of spending) and still maintain the effectiveness of the spending regulations for candidates and parties.

The *National Citizens' Coalition* case was not appealed, nor was alternative legislation enacted.[7] Although the decision applied only to Alberta, Joseph Gorman, the Commissioner of Canada Elections, decided that interest group election spending would not be prosecuted anywhere in the country. The reason given by Huguette Collins, Gorman's former administrative assistant, was that it would be unconscionable in a federal election to subject people in one province to one set of regulations whereas elsewhere in the country they were subject to different rules. Although there have been two federal elections conducted since this decision was made, the 1984 election did not result in significant interest group spending. This is not surprising given that the timing of the decision not to enforce the legislation (which occurred during the actual election period) probably created uncertainties and organizational problems for interest groups.

Federal Election (1988)

The 1988 election campaign included substantial participation by groups other than political parties. Independent expenditures by interest groups, individuals, corporations and labour unions were in excess of $4.7 million. The major sponsors of independent spending were the Canadian Alliance for Trade and Job Opportunities, the Pro-Canada Network, the National Citizens' Coalition, the Alberta government and Campaign Life. It is difficult to establish the precise extent of independent expenditures during this election because, in light of the decision not to enforce the spending regulations,[8] election spending of those other than registered candidates and parties was not officially monitored.

It is important to emphasize that the figure of $4.7 million (table 1.1) does not represent the total amount spent by these groups, but is an approximation based on independent research, the monitoring of 14 newspapers across the country, and interviews with the principal

Table 1.1
Estimated election advertising by interest groups
(dollars)

Canadian Alliance for Trade and Job Opportunities	2 307 670
National Citizens' Coalition	150 000
Alberta government	727 000
Pro-Canada Network	752 247
Campaign Life	75 000
Other (pro–free trade, anti–free trade and unrelated issues)	717 187
Total	4 729 104

Source: Figures obtained through Commission research. Numbers based on analysis of interest group advertising, for the entire election period, in 14 newspapers (see note 9). The estimates are also based on information provided in the Audited Statement of the Canadian Alliance for Trade and Job Opportunities, Statement of Receipts and Disbursements, Year End March 31, 1989; interviews with Peter Bleyer, Political Action Co-ordinator, Pro-Canada Network, 30 August 1990 and David Somerville, National Citizens' Coalition, 6 September 1990.

Note: Does not include radio or television advertising, other than that of the Canadian Alliance for Trade and Job Opportunities, which included these expenditures in the Audited Statement of Receipts and Disbursements.

interest groups involved in the election.[9] The figure, therefore, under-estimates the amount actually spent because it does not account for smaller groups or individuals who incurred expenses, nor does it include radio or television advertisements.[10] A second important considera-tion is that these figures for interest groups are based only on advertising and do not include the value of voluntary labour, internal organiza-tional or administrative costs. For these reasons, the financial impact of interest groups was higher than the figures provided. Having men-tioned these caveats in ascertaining accurate interest group expendi-tures, however, it is not likely that the total spent on advertising was significantly higher than what is reported because spending of the prin-cipal groups involved is included in the figure.

At first glance, interest group spending seems relatively minor (table 1.2) compared with what was spent by registered candidates and parties. Interest group expenditures accounted for 8 percent of all elec-tion expenses. A more significant comparison of interest group expen-ditures is with the advertising expenses for parties and candidates. This comparison is more meaningful because the interest group figure rep-resents advertising expenditures. Table 1.3 reveals that interest groups spent 40 percent of the amount the three principal parties spent on advertising.

Table 1.2
Election expenses of candidates, parties and interest groups

	Amount spent	%
Candidates	31 341 404	54
Parties	22 425 849	38
Interest groups	4 729 104	8
Total	58 496 357	100

Source: Canada, Elections Canada (1988) and Commission research.

Table 1.3
Interest group advertising as a proportion of party advertising
(dollars)

Party advertising (PC, Liberal, NDP)	11 705 209
Interest group advertising	4 729 104
Interest group advertising as a proportion of party advertising	.40

Source: Canada, Elections Canada (1988) and Commission research.

Table 1.4
Comparison of pro–free trade and PC party and candidate advertising
(dollars)

Canadian Alliance for Trade and Job Opportunities	2 307 670
Government of Alberta	727 000
National Citizens' Coalition	150 000
Other pro–free trade	454 234
Total pro–free trade expenditures	3 638 904
PC party advertising	4 716 737
PC candidate advertising	7 462 877
Total PC advertising	12 179 614
Amount of pro–free trade advertising for every $1.00 of PC party and candidate advertising	0.30

Source: Canada, Elections Canada (1988) and Commission research.

Table 1.5
Comparison of anti–free trade and Liberal/NDP party and candidate advertising
(dollars)

Pro-Canada Network	752 247
Other anti–free trade	126 101
Total anti–free trade expenditures	878 348
Liberal party advertising	3 860 286
Liberal candidate advertising	5 857 051
Total	9 717 337
Amount of anti–free trade advertising for every $1.00 of Liberal party and candidate advertising	0.09
NDP advertising	3 128 186
NDP candidate advertising	3 413 027
Total	6 541 213
Amount of anti–free trade advertising for every $1.00 of NDP and candidate advertising	0.13
Amount of anti–free trade advertising for every $1.00 of all Liberal and NDP party and candidate advertising	0.05

Source: Canada, Elections Canada (1988) and Commission research.

Tables 1.4 and 1.5 suggest that the expenditures of interest groups were not evenly divided on the basis of issue. Independent advertising concentrated largely on the issue of free trade, of which expenditures promoting free trade were in excess of four times the amount spent opposing free trade. Because the Conservative party was the only one of the three to promote free trade, independent expenditures in favour of its central issue were considerably more significant than the anti–

free trade advertising campaigns for the Liberal or NDP parties.

The Conservative advertising effort (both by candidates and parties) benefited from independent expenditures to promote free trade in the amount of $0.30 for every advertising dollar the party itself spent. In contrast, each dollar of combined Liberal and NDP advertising was supplemented by $0.05 from anti–free trade supporters. It is important to emphasize that in assessing these figures, what is being compared is not how much interest groups spent to promote or oppose free trade in relation to what the parties spent on that same issue. The advertising figures for the parties include their total expenditures for all advertising. While these tables provide an indication of the relative significance of interest group advertisements in relation to the particular parties, the most revealing figures are those contained in table 1.6, which approximates this relationship at the national level. The overwhelming majority of interest group expenditures were associated with national campaigns either for or against free trade. Similarly, the focus of the free trade debate at the partisan level was at the national party level, rather than the candidate level. Table 1.6 illustrates that pro–free trade groups spent $0.77 for every $1.00 of the Conservative party advertising budget, while anti–free trade forces spent only $0.13 for every dollar spent by the two political parties opposing free trade.

Independent expenditures in the 1988 election undermined the principles of fairness and equity. The benefits of interest group advertisements, in terms of which issues were favourably promoted, disproportionately accrued to one party. At the national level, the Conservative party received almost four times the independent financial support promoting free trade (the central issue in the party's campaign plank) than the Liberal or NDP parties received from anti–free trade groups. While there was no indication that the Alliance spending was coordinated in any way with PC efforts to promote free trade, table 1.6 suggests that fairness and equity were undermined even in the absence of collusion or coordination.

Table 1.6
Free trade expenditures as proportion of party advertising
(dollars)

Amount of pro–free trade advertising for every $1.00 of PC party advertising	0.77
Amount of anti–free trade advertising for every $1.00 of Liberal party advertising	0.23
Amount of anti–free trade advertising for every $1.00 of NDP advertising	0.28
Amount of anti–free trade advertising for every $1.00 of Liberal and NDP advertising	0.13

Source: Canada, Elections Canada (1988) and Commission research.

It is not just the amount or content of interest group advertising that had an impact on candidates and parties during the election. The timing of the advertisements is also significant because of the dynamics of voters' support during the similar period. Support for the Conservatives plunged between 25 and 28 October immediately following the televised leadership debates (the French debate was on the twenty-fourth while the English was on the twenty-fifth), whereas Liberal support surged. The Liberals may even have assumed the lead by mid-November, but as late as the second last weekend of the campaign, the numbers were too close to call. During the final week of the campaign something happened: a significant shift in support occurred in which the Conservatives recovered (Johnston 1990).

It was during this recovery period that the overwhelming majority of interest group advertisements occurred. Earlier in October, when polls indicated the Conservative party was strong, there were virtually no advertisements placed. But early in November, as the polls showed that the Conservatives were clearly in trouble, there was a significant shift in the volume of advertising in the 14 newspapers identified earlier. In the first week of November, the average daily placement of advertisements was just under 250 000 mm^2 (the average newspaper page is about 120 000 mm^2), the equivalent of about two full pages of advertising. In the second week of November (7–13) this grew by about half to 375 000 mm^2 or three full pages. In the final week of the election came an order-of-magnitude shift. During the period 14–20 November, interest group advertisements averaged almost 1.2 million mm^2 or 10 pages per day. A significant fraction of this came on the last full circulation day, Saturday 19 November, with more than 3.1 million mm^2 of advertising, the equivalent of about 27 pages or almost two pages in each of the 14 newspapers analysed on that one day (see figure 1.1). Approximately 65 percent of the total interest group advertisement space was purchased in the last week of the campaign, of which the final full circulation day alone accounted for 25 percent (Johnston 1990).

While interest group advertisements mirrored the general Conservative recovery period, campaign trends identified in the Canadian National Election Study survey, in published polls and in media news coverage, suggest that there was not a strong correlation between either party advertisements or movements in popular support/opposition to the free trade agreement on the one hand and changes in the Conservative and Liberal shares of vote intention on the other (Johnston 1990).

In light of this, the coincidence of the surge of interest group advertisements with the last week Conservative recovery invites the question:

Figure 1.1
Net pro–free trade (FTA) newspaper advertising by interest groups
(Net = Pro-FTA – Anti-FTA)
number of pages

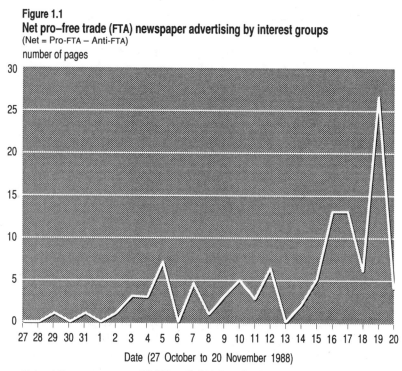

Date (27 October to 20 November 1988)

Notes: 1 Newspaper page = 120 000 mm². 1988 Canadian Election Study Newspaper Archive.
See headnote.

to what degree was this interest group advertising responsible? A study of the impact of interest group advertisements on vote intention concludes that the flood of this advertising at the end of the election did, in fact, have a modest effect on voters' intentions. While this impact is not sufficient to explain the 12 percent gap in the final popular vote for the Conservative and Liberal parties, it does, nevertheless, suggest that the promotion of issues influenced voting intentions. The last week of advertisements resulted in a net five and one-half point change in voters' intention. The Conservative party gained three points while the Liberal party lost two and one-half points.[11] This shift is not explained by new public support for free trade. Rather, the more significant impact was among respondents who already supported the Free Trade Agreement. The principal effect of the advertisements was to mobilize those Free Trade Agreement supporters intending to vote for the Liberal party to support the Conservative party (Johnston 1990).

Profile of Interest Groups Involved in Federal Election (1988)

Canadian Alliance for Trade and Job Opportunities

The largest independent expenditures were incurred by the Canadian Alliance for Trade and Job Opportunities, a coalition of business organizations, which spent $2.3 million on advertising during the election.[12] Most of the advertising was contained in newspapers, although a related Quebec-based group, whose expenditures of close to $100 000 were included in the Alliance total, used television advertising in Montreal.[13] The Alliance's advertising campaign, which occurred in the last two weeks of the election, was its second; it spent $1.7 million between April 1987 and the end of March 1988.[14]

The Alliance was formed in March 1987 as a nonpartisan advocacy group to build national support for the Free Trade Agreement. The principal means of promoting free trade included the recruitment of community and business leaders, employee programs within member organizations, print and television advertising, a communications package, participation in public television shows, and public speeches.[15]

The Alliance is best known for its newspaper advertisements, including the widely circulated four-page insert "Straight Talk on Free Trade" which was distributed at least twice in 42 daily newspapers, two weeklies and one national magazine (Canadian Alliance 1989, 8). Members of the Alliance initially had no intention of becoming financially involved during the 1988 campaign, but intervened following the leaders debate as "an attempt to save the Agreement" (ibid.). The advertising did not mention the Conservative party or any candidate, including the prime minister, and confined its message to information on the free trade issue. In no advertisement was the reader exhorted to vote for the Conservative party or to vote explicitly for free trade.

Although the two advertising campaigns (before and during the election) account for the majority of the $5.25 million that the organization had raised from corporations and individuals, the Alliance also spent $425 000 on consulting fees and close to $20 000 on salaries.[16] No attempt was made to attach a retail price to the voluntary efforts of members, many of whom were high-profile men and women from the business community who participated in an extensive two-year speaking tour, including more than 100 engagements or media interviews during the electoral period (Canadian Alliance 1989, 182).

Pro-Canada Network

The second largest independent expenditure came from the Pro-Canada Network, a coalition of individuals and organizations opposed to free trade. The Pro-Canada Network was formed in spring 1987 for the express purpose of opposing free trade (Bleyer 1990). The principal advertising activity of the organization was producing and distributing a comic book entitled "What's the Big Deal?" Most of the 2.2 million copies printed (in both English and French) were distributed in 24 national daily newspapers. The colour comic book was the single most expensive activity of the group even though much of what was required to make the book – illustrations by Terry Mosher (Aislin), writing by Rick Salutin, the design and even the paper for printing – were donated.[17] The cost of making and distributing the comic book was about $688 000, a significant portion of the organization's total expenditures of about $752 000 (Traynor 1990). Most of the money raised came from member groups, largely, although not exclusively, union based, which solicited contributions to oppose free trade (Salutin 1989, 260).[18] In addition to these organizations, a number of prominent Canadians including author Margaret Atwood and broadcaster Adrienne Clarkson helped organize telephone campaign drives (ibid., 33). Aside from the comic book, the Network sponsored a full-page newspaper advertisement and received a complimentary two-page magazine advertisement.[19]

National Citizens' Coalition

Unlike the Canadian Alliance for Trade and Job Opportunities or the Pro-Canada Network, the National Citizens' Coalition was not formed to take a stand on the free trade issue. The Coalition (NCC) was founded in 1967 and has a membership of about 40 000 (half of the Coalition's support comes from Ontario with considerable strength in Alberta and British Columbia as well). The Coalition has established a reputation as one of the principal interest groups involved in elections. The Coalition is an ideological group dedicated to promoting free enterprise and opposing government regulations in the economy. The issue of whether interest groups should participate in federal elections has become a central issue in the NCC's philosophical plank: more freedom through less government (Somerville 1990).

The NCC conducted two political advertising campaigns in 1988. The campaign that Canadians are most familiar with was the negative campaign which targeted NDP leader Ed Broadbent as an "unworthy" candidate for prime minister. The campaign actually occurred between August and October, before the election call.[20] In all, $700 000 was spent in a combination of direct mail and newspaper and radio advertisements depicting the former leader as a "scary socialist" and equating the possibility of Broadbent becoming prime minister with a "nightmare."

The actual election spending of the National Citizens' Coalition was more modest and focused on the free trade issue. In its advertising campaign, conducted in November, the Coalition spent $150 000 to promote free trade (Somerville 1990). The advertisement criticized Broadbent and Liberal leader John Turner for not supporting free trade, describing Broadbent as being "very, very scary" and suggesting that as a "dedicated socialist" he did not believe in free enterprise. The advertisement also criticized Turner, suggesting that he was a "professional politician" whose position on the issue should not be given serious consideration because he "says what he thinks you want to hear" (*Globe and Mail*, 18 Nov. 1988) and is in "the fight of his life to save his job, not yours" (*Toronto Star*, 20 Nov. 1988). The Coalition also engaged in a limited amount of television advertising in the Toronto region (Somerville 1990).

Campaign Life

Campaign Life Coalition, an organization which frequently relies on negative advertising, is the political wing of the pro-life movement in Canada. The group, as its name suggests, is a single issue organization dedicated to opposing policies (and their promoters) allowing for abortions. The Coalition has chapters in eight provinces and has about 40 branches across the country.

National president James Hughes defines abortion as the pivotal issue in any election campaign and suggests that the organization plays a crucial role in providing a balance to what his group calls a "biased" media (Hughes 1990). The organization compiles a record of how MPs vote on the issue, based on free votes in the House and on policy statements and responses to questionnaires submitted to candidates by Campaign Life. It uses its findings as a way of determining which candidates are "worthy" of being elected; the test is whether a candidate, under any circumstance, opposes abortion.[21]

Hughes indicates that the organization has little money (the average contribution is $30 a year) and is dependent upon "foot soldiers" – volunteers who are prepared to go door to door, urging voters to vote for candidates who oppose abortion. While the organization is non-partisan, it regularly targets NDP candidates who support the party's pro-choice position.[22] Estimates of 1988 campaign expenditures are between $75 000 and $100 000, based mostly on the publication of newsletters and pamphlets (Hughes 1990).

Alberta Government

One other significant source of independent expenditures during the election was the Alberta government which spent $727 000 between

28 October and 19 November 1988 to promote free trade within the province. The campaign included newspaper advertisements featuring prominent Albertans who supported the trade deal (12 insertions in each of the nine Alberta daily papers), 33 radio advertisements, as well as an eight-page tabloid flyer, similar in content to the Alliance advertisements (Parr 1990) delivered to 836 000 households in the province (Salutin 1989, 125).

Ontario Provincial Election (1990)

Four interest groups engaged in independent expenditures, largely directed at opposing the incumbent Liberal government, headed by David Peterson. The largest expenditures came from the Ontario Medical Association, which spent approximately $500 000 in direct mail, radio advertisements and media events demanding an end to cut-backs in health care. The literature did not explicitly direct readers to vote against the Liberal government, but the message was clear that the Liberal government was responsible for undermining health care. Aside from the literature and advertisements, including radio advertisements costing $300 000 in the last two weeks of the campaign (Rhodes 1990), the Association staged a skit with professional actors criticizing hospital cut-backs (*Globe and Mail*, 4 Sept. 1990, A6).[23]

Equally critical of the Liberal government was the Ontario Secondary School Teachers' Federation which spent about $250 000 on billboards, brochures and two newspaper advertisements focusing on underfunding of education (French 1990). The key slogan of the organization was: "School Underfunding is Child Neglect."

The Canadian Auto Workers (CAW) engaged in a number of election activities including advertisements in three newspapers (criticizing plant closures), the circulation of pamphlets at workplaces and the organization of a march from Windsor to Peterson's London campaign office. The march included a float with free trade depicted as the grim reaper, 60 workers with tombstones symbolizing plant closures and a six-foot puppet of David Peterson. The CAW has not revealed how much it spent on election activities (Harrison 1990). The fourth group active in the election was the National Citizens' Coalition (NCC) which advertised concern about taxes in newspapers and pamphlets (Nicholls 1991).[24]

COMPARATIVE EXPERIENCE

Three provinces have addressed the issue of interest group electoral participation with varying levels of restrictions on political expression. Interest groups or individuals other than registered candidates have almost no opportunity to spend money to promote policy issues in Quebec. In Nova Scotia, independent expenditures cannot be directed at candidate/party names and cannot promote issues on which candidates or parties have assumed positions. The least restrictive regime is the one in Saskatchewan where groups can readily avail themselves of a defence from prosecution and potentially can engage in almost any kind of activity (promoting both issues and identifying candidate or party names) short of coordination or collusion with candidates or parties.

Quebec

The Quebec *Election Act* provides for the most restrictive of the provincial regimes, in terms of the ability of interest groups or other non-registered participants to advertise during elections. During elections in Quebec, only the official agent of a party or candidate may authorize election expenses (*Election Act*, s. 413). The definition of election expenses is more inclusive than in most other Canadian jurisdictions and includes almost all goods and services used to promote or oppose, directly or indirectly, a candidate or party and issues or programs of a candidate or party.[25]

In addition to prohibiting groups or individuals from incurring election expenses, there have been two incidents in which Quebec election officials have asked that the publication of books which focused attention on candidates or parties be delayed until after an election. In 1985 a candidate who was the author of such a book was asked by Quebec election officials either to include the cost of publicity in his election expenses or to delay the publication. He did the latter. In another case, a political science professor complied with a request to delay the publication of a book that discussed the program of a political party (Barry 1990).

Enforcement proceedings against violations have usually resulted in an admission of guilt by the parties and compliance with formal notices to abandon advertisement campaigns before legal proceedings were begun. For example, in 1985 Quebec's Chief Electoral Officer Pierre Côté persuaded three unions or professional associations to stop broadcasting advertisements or distributing pamphlets denouncing certain government policies. In the last provincial election campaign, Côté issued more than 30 official notices to stop advertising, and all complied (Côté 1989, 21–22).

The law, to date, has been upheld against rights-based challenges. These sections of the law, which were enacted in 1989, are essentially the same as those involved in two notable 1982 court judgements in which the Quebec Superior Court found that the legislation did not violate freedom of expression in the Quebec *Charter of Human Rights and Freedoms.* In both cases the Court rejected arguments that freedom of expression requires the ability to spend money to promote issues; expression cannot be equated with spending money (*Roberge* 1980; *Boucher* 1982).

The legislation, which is more restrictive than the federal law successfully challenged by the *National Citizens' Coalition* case, has not been subject to a challenge on the basis of the *Canadian Charter of Rights and Freedoms.* There is reason to question, however, whether the legislation would survive a Charter challenge before the Supreme Court of Canada. The basis for the two Quebec decisions upholding the legislation has been that the law imposed no restriction on freedom of expression. The judicial assumption has been that freedom of expression protects only the right of expression, not the right to spend money to advocate views. This approach to assessing rights-based claims is conceptually different from that of the Supreme Court. The Supreme Court has generally found that rights should be interpreted initially in a broad manner. It has rejected the position that freedom of expression should be interpreted in light of the content (for example, whether it is hate propaganda or not) or in light of the particular context in which it arose (whether expression was of a commercial nature). Furthermore, the Court has indicated that it will not be easily convinced of the justification for limits on free speech (*Keegstra* 1990, 66) and that the government assumes the burden for demonstrating that its reason for limiting the protected right was justified. At this stage, the Quebec government would have difficulty convincing the Court that no less restrictive means were available to maintain the integrity of candidate or party spending limits.

Nova Scotia
Under Nova Scotia legislation, only official agents or authorized representatives of a candidate or party can incur election expenses, which are defined as all expenses for the purpose of "promoting or opposing directly or indirectly the election of a candidate, or a person who becomes or is likely to become a candidate, or the program or policy of a candidate or party" (Nova Scotia *Elections Act*, s. 3(i)). Election expenses include expenditures incurred for literature or objects or materials of an advertising nature used to promote or oppose a candidate.[26]

While the legislation, on its face, seems similar to the 1983 federal legislation, there is one important difference. The scope of the prohibitions in Nova Scotia is considerably broader. The law precludes interest groups from advocating positions on issues that have been raised in the campaign of a candidate or party. This suggests that as soon as any party or candidate makes a statement on an issue of policy, interest groups are legally barred from incurring expenses to promote their position on that issue. Taken to its extreme, if candidates or parties were to take positions on all relevant policy issues, there would be no opportunity for interest groups to advertise policy views. While there is some doubt as to whether this provision would survive a constitutional challenge (the discussion above suggested the Supreme Court would likely require some demonstration that less intrusive measures were available), as yet there has not been any litigation concerning this aspect of the law. Although there have been minor incidents involving signs that advocated the defeat of specific candidates, these activities stopped as soon as the organizers were advised that they were violating the law (Ferguson 1990).

Saskatchewan
The Saskatchewan law on the involvement of interest groups in elections is the least restrictive of the three provincial regimes and is similar to the federal law before the good faith defence was repealed in 1983. The legislation provides that no one other than a candidate, his or her agent, or the agent of a registered party can incur election expenses, which are defined as expenses used "for the purpose of promoting or opposing, directly or indirectly during an election, a particular registered party or the election of a particular candidate ... " (Saskatchewan *The Election Act*, s. 231(1)). The legislation contains a defence from prosecution, however, which makes it difficult to prevent groups from incurring election expenses that promote or oppose candidates. The defence is invoked if the accused can establish that the expenses were incurred:

(a) for the purpose of gaining support for views held by him on an issue of public policy, or for the purpose of advancing the aims of any organization or association, other than a political party or an organization or association of a partisan political character, of which he was a member and on whose behalf the expenses were incurred; and

(b) in good faith and not for any purpose related to the provisions of this Act limiting the amount of election expenses that may be incurred by any other person. (Saskatchewan *The Election Act*, s. 231(4))

Like the federal law prior to 1983, the Saskatchewan law makes it difficult to limit the activities of interest groups. One interpretation of the law is that, because the good faith defence exempts individuals or groups from being prosecuted for incurring election expenses (which are defined as expenses incurred to promote or oppose a candidate or party), the defence allows them to promote or oppose candidates or parties. Except for incidents of collusion where an individual or group has essentially acted as a front for a political party or candidate as a way of supplementing the legal limit, it is difficult to imagine situations in which groups could not argue that they were promoting an issue of policy or advancing their organizations' aims or objectives. This interpretation is supported by the *Roach* trial and appeal decisions.

An alternative interpretation of the good faith defence, although less persuasive, accords a far more limited role to interest groups. It suggests that they can promote policy issues but cannot identify the names of candidates or parties. The rationale for this argument focuses on the section in the provision which links the good faith defence to the requirement that advertising must not relate to the provisions limiting the amount of election expenses that may be incurred by any other person (Lampard 1990).[27]

Not surprisingly, in light of the wide net cast for defence from prosecution of the legislation, there have been few incidents in which groups have engaged in activities that were not entitled to the defence. A number of advertisements and pamphlets that appeared during two 1988 by-elections prompted election officials to consider prosecution, but in fact no prosecutions took place. Consideration to prosecute was not so much a result of the content of the advertisements themselves but rather an attempt to subject the provisions to judicial review as a means of clarifying the intent of the legislation.[28] There have been no judicial interpretations of this aspect of the Saskatchewan law. A commissioner was appointed to study the issue but his report has not been made public (Lampard 1990).

Great Britain
The central feature of the regulatory regime reflects the assumption that elections are contests between individual candidates. This is provided for in section 75 of the *Representation of the People Act*, which stipulates that no one other than the candidate (who is subject to spending limits) or his or her agents shall spend money "with a view to promoting or procuring the election of a candidate." One of the consequences of this focus on candidates is that interest groups are effectively precluded from incurring expenditures at the constituency level. Furthermore, Britain has a ban on all paid political advertising on television and radio. The fact that interest groups (as well as candidates

and parties) cannot advertise on the broadcast media means newspapers are the principal forum for independent expenditures.

Interest group election activity, particularly at the local level, is strictly enforced. While the legislation does not formally prohibit interest groups from engaging in negative advertising and does not explicitly address the question of whether they can link candidates' names to the promotion of issues, judicial enforcement of the spirit as well as the letter of the regulatory framework has limited the scope of interest group activities. For example, in the *Hailwood and Ackroyd* case (1928), negative campaigning by an interest group against one candidate was taken as promoting the election of the others and hence prohibited (Ewing 1987, 91).

Interest group advertisements during elections are common at the national level. The legislation does not address the issue of whether interest groups can financially promote a party (it restricts only the promotion of candidates). Interest group advertisements have both promoted issues and opposed parties. Notable examples of involvement of interest groups are the 1959 anti-nationalization campaign where the iron and steel lobby spent more than the total expenses of all candidates and four times more on advertising than the Conservative party, which also opposed nationalization (Butler and Rose 1960). In a more recent example, the 1983 election, a number of groups critical of the government's record on employment spent an estimated £1.2 million, more than the advertising expenditure of the Labour Party which stood to benefit from the anti-government campaign (Pinto-Duschinsky 1989, 39–41).

Judicial interpretations of spending efforts of interest groups have determined that advertising campaigns which identify parties are, in fact, legal. Unlike the *Hailwood and Ackroyd* example where courts determined that indirect advertisements – those, for example which explicitly opposed a particular candidate – must be considered as promoting candidates and are therefore illegal, the courts have not found similarly that advertisements promoting parties also indirectly promote candidates. For example, in the *Tronah Mines* case (1952), the advertisement in question urged election of a party other than Labour. The advertisement was not found to be "presenting to the electors of any constituency any particular candidate" and, therefore, did not have the effect of supporting non-Labour candidates (Ewing 1987, 95).

France
The principle guiding the French electoral regime is equality of treatment of candidates. The core assumption in the regulatory regime is

that the way of achieving this is through extensive and detailed regulations and public funding for campaign brochures and posters, public allocation of free broadcast time, and a ban on paid political advertising during the election in newspapers, radio and television. While the parties are provided with free broadcast time, there is a ban in the last week of the campaign on the diffusion of or commentary on all polls involving candidates or issues in the electoral debate. Not surprisingly, in light of these regulations (in particular, the ban on media advertising), interest groups have not assumed a significant role in elections. The regulatory framework allows few avenues for participation other than the official campaigns of candidates and parties. For example, in one of the few references to involvement of interest groups in the election literature, interventions such as a statement by a bishop ordering his following not to vote for communists, or the Chamber of Agriculture suggesting that its members vote for professionals in the agricultural industry, have been held to be contrary to the regulations (Masclet 1989).

United States

The contemporary American experience with participation of interest groups in elections (Political Action Committees, commonly referred to as PACs)[29] has been largely driven by a series of legislative reforms. The reforms of the election regulatory regime were spurred by revelations uncovered by Watergate-related investigations of the impact of special interest groups and wealthy contributors in the electoral process. The goals of the *Federal Election Campaign Act* (FECA) enacted in 1971 were to "render the media more accessible and less expensive to candidates for federal office" and to "obtain broad disclosure of federal campaign funds" in an attempt to discourage the solicitation and acceptance of large sums of money from single contributors. The objective of reducing expenses and, therefore, the potential for corruption and undue influence arising from money, was to be attained through a detailed series of limits on candidates' advertising expenditures (Matasar 1986, 9).

While corporations and unions are formally prohibited from directly spending money to advocate the election or defeat of a candidate or party,[30] they participate in elections by making contributions through PACs. A number of legislative and judicial developments have contributed to the growth of PACs. Legislation in 1971 enabling corporations and unions to use general treasury funds to establish and administer PACs (Alexander 1984, 89–90)[31] when combined with a 1974 amendment that lifted the restriction on firms with government contracts to contribute in elections, meant that corporations and unions could create PACs without threat of losing government work (Alexander 1984; Mutch 1988, 170–71).[32] If there were any lingering doubts about possible repercussions from establishing PACs, a Federal Election Commission (FEC) advisory opinion (the *Sun-Pac* case) in 1975, which allowed corporate PACs to solicit employees, removed all questions about the ability of corporations with government contracts to utilize PACs (Matasar 1986, 12).

An important contributing factor to the development of PACs, in particular corporate PACs, was the creation of a two-tiered approach to campaign contributions (Matasar 1986, 11). While individuals are allowed to contribute $1 000 to any candidate for federal office and $25 000 to all federal candidates and committees per year in the aggregate, multi-candidate PACs have considerably higher contribution limits to individual candidates ($5 000) and have no aggregate contribution limit.[33] The impact of these legislative initiatives on the growth of PACs is evident in the sheer volume of these groups. PACs grew in number from 113 in 1972 to 4 828 by 1988 (Magleby and Nelson 1990, 74).

While this growth of PACs is an important part of the explanation for why they have assumed such a large role in American elections, the American experience cannot fully be understood without analysing the interplay of these legislative initiatives with judicial review of campaign finance reforms. A number of Supreme Court decisions have had significant implications for PAC participation in federal elections. The most important of these was *Buckley v. Valeo* (1976), which severely undermined the objective of the 1974 reforms to reduce the costs of contesting elections. What was significant for the role of PACs was the Court's ruling that limits on independent expenditures by individuals and committees are unconstitutional, but ceilings on contributions for individuals and PACs are valid.

Independent Expenditures

The impugned legislation had prohibited individuals or groups from incurring any "expenditure ... relative to a clearly identified candidate during a calendar year which, when added to all other expenditures ... advocating the election or defeat of such candidate, exceeds $1,000" (*Buckley* 1976, 42).

The most serious shortcoming of the legislation indicated by the Court was the assumption that the speech of some elements of society should be restricted in order to enhance the relative voice of others. In the view of the Court, the First Amendment's protection against governmental abridgement of free expression cannot be dependent on a person's financial ability to engage in public discussion: "The concept that government may restrict the speech of some elements of our society in order to enhance the relative voice of others is wholly foreign to the First Amendment, which was designed 'to secure "the widest possible dissemination of information from diverse and antagonistic sources"' and '"to assure unfettered interchange of ideas for the bringing about of political and social changes desired by the people"'" (ibid., 49).[34]

Contribution Limits

The contribution limits for PACs fared better, as the Court held that contribution ceilings do not generate as great an impairment of free speech as do limits on independent expenditures:

> By contrast with a limitation upon expenditures for political expression, a limitation upon the amount that any one person or group may contribute to a candidate or political committee entails only a marginal restriction upon the contributor's ability to engage in free communication. A contribution serves as a general expression of support for the candidate and his views, but does not communicate the underlying basis for the support. The quantity of communication by the contributor does not increase perceptibly with the size of his contribution, since the expression rests solely on the undifferentiated, symbolic act of contributing. At most, the size of the contribution provides a very rough index of the intensity of the contributor's support for the candidate. A limitation on the amount of money a person may give to a candidate or campaign organization thus involves little direct restraint on his political communication, for it permits the symbolic expression of support evidenced by a contribution but does not in any way infringe the contributor's freedom to discuss candidates and issues. (*Buckley* 1976, 20–21)

Another aspect of *Buckley v. Valeo* had important implications for elections. The legislation had set spending ceilings on candidates seeking election to the House of Representatives, the Senate and presidency.[35] The Court found that no governmental interest was sufficient to "justify the restriction on the quantity of political expression" imposed by the legislation. In its view, the danger of a candidate's dependency on large contributions – the major evil associated with rapidly increasing campaign expenditures – was served by contribution limits and disclosure provisions rather than campaign expenditure ceilings (*Buckley* 1976, 55).

An important consequence of the Court's decision to reject expenditure ceilings for candidates is that PACs have assumed an important role as sources of funding for congressional campaigns, particularly for the House of Representatives (Conway 1983, 131).[36]

Assessments of PAC Influence

Since the 1976 decision, the cost of House and Senate elections has spiralled above the inflation rate, prompting suggestions that PACs are largely responsible for this phenomenon. PAC contributions to congressional candidates have increased from $23 million in 1976 ($17 million in constant 1972 dollars) to $147.9 million in 1988 ($52 million in constant 1972 dollars) (United States, FEC 1989). Despite the significant increase in the costs of elections and in the amounts contributed to candidates by PACs, it is misleading to suggest the significance of special interest money in elections is due to PACs. Criticisms of the claim that PACs are the principal reason for the increased costs in elections focus on the assumption that PAC contributions represent proportionately more interest group money than they did prior to the amendments in the 1970s. While the PAC structure grew out of the amendments of the 1970s, special interest money in elections is not a new phenomenon but was one of the principal reasons for the legislative reforms. What PACs have contributed to the electoral process is greater transparency for the financial role of individuals and groups. By requiring that disclosures must be made by those who contribute to parties fully and regularly, PACs have replaced a system which was heavily weighted in favour of "anonymous" concentrated and special interest money by a system in which contributions are more broadly dispersed and are transparent (Sabato 1990, 188–89).

What generates cynicism is the perception that, as agents of interest groups, PACs' financial contributions result in special privileges or favours and, in the extreme, in elections being "bought and sold." Many of the concerns of the role of PACs in elections are similar to those revealed in the discussion of interest groups, while other criticisms are a result of the peculiar role of PACs in the American political system.

One issue that generates sharp debate and reflects differing assumptions about the nature of representation is whether PACs contribute to, or detract from, the democratic nature of the political process. Supporters of PACs, like defenders of interest group election participation in Canada, argue that these groups contribute information and knowledge to the electoral debate and assume roles that parties are either unwilling to perform or are incapable of performing (Matasar 1986, 4).[37] Opponents see their contribution in a far less benign manner. They argue that PACs do not enhance representation and accountability because incumbents increasingly rely on PACs for campaign contributions and are thus more accountable to and concerned about PACs' interests than those of voters (Grenzke 1990, 143).

> Even when PACs do not focus mainly on obtaining direct economic benefits, they create a problem for representative government. Because money is transferable, PACs nationalize funding sources. They collect ample treasuries in small individual gifts from many locales, centralize those funds in the hands of institutional officers, and make large contributions in strategically important races anywhere in the country. The real and effective financial constituency in these circumstances is the PAC and its leadership, not the small givers to campaign warchests. The candidate knows the programs and objectives of the PAC, and it is to the PAC officers that preferred access is given. These nationally centralized institutions thus compete with local constituents ... for the attention of public officials ... It is difficult to be sanguine about their adverse effects on political competition and accountability, on economic, ideological, and partisan balances, and on the policy-making process. More than a minor threat to democratic politics has accompanied whatever happy consequences have flowed from the emergence of PACs. (Adamany 1980, 596–97. Copyright ©1980 by the Arizona Board of Regents. Reprinted by permission.)

Another important debate is whether PAC contributions lead to undue influence. Political commentators do not dispute the fact that, as a result of their importance in raising campaign funds, particularly for House of Representatives candidates, PACs enjoy access to decision makers that might otherwise be denied to them. Some commentators interpret this access as granting special consideration in the policy process. In reaching this conclusion, they focus largely on the coincidence of congressional roll-call votes and PAC contributions (Drew 1983; Common Cause 1981, 1984, 1986). One complaint with the assumption that access translates into undue influence is that it fails to consider lobbying efforts and therefore exaggerates the influence of contributions (Wright 1990, 418). Another criticism is that this interpretation dismisses the fact that congressional representatives vote according to constituency pressures, party pressures, and their own ideology; they would, in short, vote in a similar manner without PAC money. The coincidence of PAC support with voting records reflects little more than the fact that PACs identify candidates with views similar to their own and then contribute money to help re-elect supporters (Grenzke 1990, 144).

Another concern with special interest money, particularly independent expenditures, is that while candidates must assume responsibility for the manner in which they spend money obtained from direct contributions and they can thus be held accountable by voters, there is no such parallel for independent expenditures. "The bulk of such spending is made by a small number of unaffiliated, ideological PACs that have no parent organization – such as unions, corporations or trade and professional associations – and solicit the public primarily through direct mail appeals. With no sponsoring organization to accept responsibility, and with contributors scattered across the country, those who make direct independent expenditures may be tempted to engage in activities that verge on excess" (Twentieth Century Fund 1984, 7).

Another criticism of PACs is that they favour established candidates by enhancing an already strong incumbency advantage and decreasing the possibility of competitive election campaigns (Alexander 1984, 103). The rate of re-election in the 1988 election was 98 percent, an election in which three-quarters of PAC contributions went to incumbents (Magleby and Nelson 1990, 54).

In explaining the preference of PACs to contribute to incumbents, many commentators suggest it is not surprising that PACs are reluctant to give money to candidates who appear to have little chance of winning. Individual donors also display a preference for incumbents. As one commentator asks: "Why waste money on non-incumbents if incumbents almost always win?" (Sabato 1987, 158). Furthermore, the mere fact of incumbency does not guarantee a PAC contribution. Other factors such as ideology, party affiliation, candidate need, the location of the corporate facility or union local in the district, and the competitiveness of the race are important factors in affecting PAC decisions to contribute (Alexander 1984, 104).

Impact of Judicial Review on Regulating PAC Activities

While the *Buckley* decision greatly increased the financial importance of PAC contributions by nullifying spending limits for candidates, a number of other decisions have directly affected the role of PACs. These decisions affect the ability to regulate the nature and, in some cases, the amount of PAC spending. An understanding of what is acceptable campaign participation is not readily apparent: the legislative standards themselves are vague and judicial review further creates doubts about what is and what is not legally and constitutionally acceptable.

This confusion is most pronounced in connection with the distinction between the express advocacy of candidates and the promotion of political issues. Such a distinction is particularly important because it affects the scope of corporate election involvement as well as the regulatory impact on independent expenditures. Corporations, for example, can make unlimited independent expenditures to promote issues but cannot directly incur expenditures deemed to constitute express partisan advocacy. Judicial review has largely merged the two activities; however, it brings into question whether advertisements that advocate a policy issue by way of promoting or opposing a candidate are in fact issue advocacy and therefore constitute allowable corporate or union election activities. This merging also calls into question the significance of contribution limits for PACs if they can spend money independently in ways that appear to promote candidates rather than merely advocate issues.

The practice of preventing corporations from directly promoting candidates in elections reflects the belief that "resources amassed in the economic marketplace" can be used to obtain "an unfair advantage in the political marketplace" (MCFL 1986, 257). Following from this principle and the legislative developments in the 1970s, the only way corporations could financially participate in elections was through the formation of PACs. But a number of recent court developments have confused the issue of what is allowable activity by corporations and unions during an election.

There are two reasons for this uncertainty: judicial developments that have changed the understanding of the kind of activities in which corporations can engage, and the softening of the distinction between express partisan advocacy and issue advocacy. The Supreme Court has expanded the opportunities for corporate election participation by establishing the principle that the First Amendment protects speech, even when its source is a corporation (*First National Bank* 1978, 789–90) and by ruling that non-economic corporations can make independent political expenditures without establishing PACs (MCFL 1986, 265–66).[38]

These developments, when combined with a softening of the distinction between express partisan advocacy and issue advocacy, have significantly enhanced the range of election activities in which corporations and unions can engage. Despite early indications that judicial definitions of express advocacy constituted such exhortations to vote for or against candidates as "vote for," "elect," "support," "cast your ballot for," "Smith for Congress," "vote against," "defeat" or "reject" (*Buckley* 1976, 44), subsequent judicial decisions have blurred the distinction between express partisan advocacy and issue advocacy. In responding to ongoing challenges by PACs, corporations and individuals to merge the definition of express partisan advocacy with issue advocacy, the courts, as yet, have not been able to agree on a definition that clearly distinguishes between these two forms of advertisement. A good example of this is the *Federal Election Commission v. Furgatch*, in which the United States Court of Appeals implicitly criticized the lack of a clear legislative standard on express advocacy and attempted to define its own: "Speech need not include any of the words listed in *Buckley* to be express advocacy ... but it must, when read as a whole, and with limited reference to external events, be susceptible of no other reasonable interpretation but as an exhortation to vote for or against a specific candidate" (*Furgatch* 1987, 864).

The Court articulated three standards for evaluating speech and stated that if any reasonable alternative reading of speech can be suggested, it cannot be express advocacy subject to the Act's disclosure requirements.

> [S]peech is "express" ... if its message is unmistakable and unambiguous, suggestive of only one plausible meaning. Second, speech may only be termed "advocacy" if it presents a clear plea for action, and thus speech that is merely informative is not covered ... Finally, it must be clear what action is advocated. Speech cannot be "express advocacy of the election or defeat of a clearly identified candidate" when reasonable minds could differ as to whether it encourages a vote for or against a candidate or encourages the reader to take some other kind of action. (ibid.)

Although this decision attempts to define speech according to the context in which it was made, there is still considerable room for discrepancy on the issues of whether the message presents a plea for action or what that plea is. To date, there has not been a ruling from the Supreme Court to clarify the matter.

The lack of clarity between issue advocacy and express partisan advocacy is important not only for how it affects the scope and regulation of corporate political expenditures (corporations and unions, it will be remembered, are prohibited from engaging in express partisan advocacy). It is also significant because it determines whether individual political expenditures must be disclosed. If individual expenditures are held to be in relation to the promotion of issues, no disclosure is required. If the expenditure is for express candidate advocacy, however, any expenditure over $250 must be disclosed.[39]

One consequence of the lack of clarity as to the distinction between candidate and issue advocacy is that the Federal Election Commission (which enforces the contribution limits and disclosure requirements) must tackle the issue case by case. Officials ask a number of questions in determining how to proceed, namely: who is advertising, what is the content or message of the advertisement, what is the context in which the message is conveyed, and when in the electoral cycle does the advertisement take place (Lerner 1990). The most difficult cases involve advertisements that may identify candidates either by name, picture, or both; contain a positive or derogatory statement about their position on a particular issue; state a position on that particular issue; and urge voters to make a wise, informed or educated vote. The difficulty in making a pronouncement as to whether this is candidate or issue advocacy is that the message does not explicitly exhort the voter to vote for a particular candidate (Biersack 1990).

Although the courts have played a significant role in determining the parameters of what the FEC can and cannot regulate, its ability to regulate PAC activity and corporate and union political involvement is also determined by the extent to which groups willingly comply with the regulations.

Enforcement Process

The FEC has responsibilities for making campaign finance reports available to the public, interpreting and enforcing the *Federal Election Campaign Act*, and implementing public funding of presidential elections. The most difficult of these tasks, and the one on which the FEC has received the most criticism, is enforcement.[40] Two ways that enforcement proceedings can be initiated are through complaints and information generated as a result of audits of disclosed records. In both cases the Office of the General Counsel makes a recommendation on whether or not there is reason to believe that a violation has occurred. The Commission (made up of six members, with no more than three from one party) votes on the recommendation: four votes are required to pursue the investigation.

The majority of the Commission's cases are resolved through a conciliation agreement. This is not surprising given that many of those being investigated are anxious to avoid publicity, which is heightened by litigating a matter rather than settling it through conciliation. On average, the Commission files lawsuits on less than 10 percent of the matters on review (Gross 1989, 228). The Commission relies on public complaints to enforce the financial and disclosure regulations. Roughly half of the Commission's case load is generated through public complaints (Magleby and Nelson 1990, 130). Enforcement difficulties arise from the lack of any precise definition that would distinguish partisan advocacy from issue advocacy. As a result, public complaints are helpful in recognizing and prosecuting attempts to package the advocacy of a candidate as a promotion of issues in order to bypass expenditure limits for PACs or get around prohibitions on direct corporate partisan advocacy (Lerner 1990; Biersack 1990).[41]

It is not only the vagueness of the law which hinders successful enforcement of the spirit of the regulatory regime. Many transgressions, because of the nature of the activity, are inherently difficult to detect. For example, when a corporation "requests" that employees contribute to PACs in return for a "bonus" (in other words, a reimbursement) enforcement is often dependent on disgruntled employees complaining to the FEC (Lerner 1990).[42] Similarly, when a political committee attempts to surpass its legal contribution limit by surreptitiously coordinating its activities with the campaign strategy of the intended recipient candidate and packaging these efforts as an independent expenditure, the FEC is often dependent on opposing candidates and their supporters to inform it of these activities (Biersack 1990).

Although the willingness of individuals or watchdog groups like Common Cause to press complaints is a vital aspect of enforcing many of the regulations, some critics argue that there is potential for mischief in the form of maligning a political foe:

> Ideally, opposing political forces enhance the enforcement of the FECA by monitoring each other's activities and bringing abuses to the attention of the Commission by filing a complaint. In some cases, however, candidates and political organizations are badgered about minor oversights and forced to expend valuable resources responding to complaints that ultimately result in no offense. Underfunded candidates or organizations may be forced to spend valuable resources defending frivolous complaints filed by opponents. (Gross 1989, 228–29)

A second problem with enforcement is the perception among some political participants that the benefits of violating the regulations outweigh any penalties imposed, especially if publicity generated by the investigation occurs after the election (Gross 1989, 228–29). In the opinion of one former Commissioner, people take the attitude that "the Commission is never going to get four votes, so they can do anything they want," a perception that is "undercutting what was anyway a rather weak enforcement system and making it even more toothless" (Magleby and Nelson 1990, 128).

CONSIDERATIONS FOR REFORM

While there was little disagreement among participants in the Commission's hearings that the asymmetry in the Canadian federal election finance laws needs redress,[43] there is no consensus on what the appropriate regulatory scheme should be. The particular view taken on this issue correlates strongly with one's conception of the impact of the Charter of Rights on the political process. Some commentators believe that freedom of expression, which is enshrined in section 2(b) of the Charter, is of paramount importance to all other values and should not be limited for any reason. According to this perspective, no individual or organization should be denied the opportunity to spend money to advertise his or her views. This ability to speak freely is held to be of an even greater value during elections when the ability to criticize governments and those seeking public office, without reprisal, is vitally important to the electoral process. Consequently, the objectives of a fair and equitable electoral process are not considered to be a justifiable restriction on free speech.

An alternative view recognizes that while the Charter has added an important dimension to the Constitution, it has not altered other fundamental tenets of our political system, such as the role of parties. Given the importance of parties as the bridge between state action and electors' preferences, the Charter should not be interpreted so rigidly that it adversely affects the electoral conditions in which candidates and parties compete. From this perspective, the ability of individuals or organizations to financially exercise free speech must be assessed in the context of how free speech affects the entire electoral process. The Charter has not repealed the values of fairness and equity as cornerstones of the electoral process. Because money spent independently can undermine these principles by nullifying the significance of regulations on party or candidate spending, there must be limits imposed upon the abilities of nonregistered participants to express themselves financially in elections.

Following from these two basic propositions are a number of specific options. Before exploring these options, it is important to emphasize that while it is highly likely that any system that imposes limits on freedom of expression will encourage a Charter challenge, there is a degree to which legislation can be designed with Charter requirements in mind and can therefore anticipate many of the kinds of challenges that have occurred in the United States. Two basic considerations could greatly reduce future uncertainty. The first is that the distinction be clear between what is and is not permissible; this should not be subject to competing interpretations. The second is the criterion that the Court generally requires to be convinced that limitations on freedom of expression are "demonstrably justified in a free and democratic society."

Distinctions between Issue Promotion and Candidate/Party Advocacy

The most difficult issue to address is how to distinguish between per-missible and impermissible advertising by nonregistered participants. The American experience is particularly instructive as to the difficul-ties in maintaining transparent and stable distinctions based on the cri-teria of issue versus partisan advocacy. The difficulty with the American approach is that advertisements that are legally recognized as issue advocacy (as opposed to partisan or "express" advocacy) can allow for the naming of a candidate or party, both in a positive and negative manner, to promote a particular issue. The line distinguishing issue from express advocacy has been in flux, resulting largely from judicial interpretations and from organizations and PACs attempting to extend the boundaries (bordering on exhortations to vote for or against can-didates) of what is packaged as issue advocacy.

While the constitutional challenges posed by the FEC attempts to enforce distinctions between issue and express advocacy are to some degree understandable given the litigious character of the United States, a judicially driven approach to regulating the activities of interest groups is not an attractive model for Canada. Many of the submissions to this Royal Commission stressed the need to simplify and clarify the lan-guage in the *Canada Elections Act*.[44] This would suggest that the dis-tinction between permissible and impermissible forms of advertising, both as written and as interpreted by the courts, should be easy to rec-ognize. Provincial and earlier federal attempts to define allowable activ-ities by interest groups during elections in terms of the distinction between issue and partisan advocacy were unsuccessful for reasons that were similar to the American experience. The ability to legally identify candidates in the advocacy of issues invites groups to pack-age explicit partisan advertisements in the form of issue advocacy, resulting in considerable difficulties enforcing the spirit of the law.

Further, a criticism of any attempt to distinguish issue promotion from partisan advocacy is that it denies an important aspect of free-dom of expression – the ability to link issues to candidate or party. This, in essence, was the basis for the *National Citizens' Coalition* challenge. It will be remembered that the legislation in 1983 did not prohibit interest groups from incurring expenses to promote issues. They could spend as much as they wished, as long as they did not directly pro-mote or oppose a candidate or party. There is considerable persuasion to the argument that freedom of expression during elections requires that individuals or interest groups be able to link issues with the rele-vant policy positions of candidates or parties. Voters do not vote for issues but for candidates and parties. For interest groups to be able to promote issues in a meaningful way, it is important that they link issues with candidates or parties.

The intent of the 1983 response to the dilemma of how to preserve the spending limits for candidates and parties and yet allow interest groups a significant degree of expression was to draw the line at the point of identifying the name of a candidate or party in the promotion of issues. This distinction, however, was successfully challenged in court. While the Supreme Court would likely depart significantly from the reasoning given in the *National Citizens' Coalition* decision, there is room for doubt as to whether the promotion of issues, without the ability to identify candidates and parties, would be considered sufficient protection of freedom of expression. The onus would be on the government to demonstrate that nothing short of a prohibition on interest groups' abilities to financially promote or oppose candidates or parties will ensure the integrity of the candidate or party spending limits.

Having argued, however, that there is merit to the view that a distinction between issue and partisan advocacy is both artificial and constitutionally suspect, the fact remains that it is virtually impossible to preserve the integrity of spending limits for candidates or parties, if interest groups are allowed significant opportunity to advertise positions that directly exhort voters to vote for or against a particular candidate or party.

Section 1 Considerations

Although we now have entrenched rights in the Charter and have considerable experience with constitutional challenges to legislation, it is not desirable to have the basic rules of our electoral process constantly subject to constitutional challenge and, therefore, in flux. This is especially true given the strict regulatory regime in place for candidates and parties. Any regime which limits expression will more than likely result in a constitutional challenge. This does not mean that the government should be reluctant to assume responsibility for making a difficult political decision to preserve a fair and equitable election system. What it does suggest, however, is that the reasons for limiting freedom of expression be based on principles or values deserving constitutional protection and that the means selected to achieve the objective be justified.

It is important to be clear about the reason for imposing limits on expression. The entire regulatory framework – including spending limits, disclosure and broadcast regulations – reflects the principles of fairness and equity. Any change in commitment to these values (for instance, dismantling the spending regulations for candidates and parties) would undermine the justification for limiting interest groups.

To repeat the argument made earlier in the study, there is little reason to assume that the Court would object to the principle of promoting a fair and equitable electoral process. The difficulty that can be anticipated lies in the second stage of the section 1 exercise. The criterion that the Court most often applies, and which is the most difficult to satisfy, is the least impairment requirement: did the legislation restrict freedom of expression as little as possible without undermining the significance of the candidate or party spending limits?

OPTIONS FOR CANADA

1. No Limits on Interest Groups or Individuals

Those who view freedom of expression, particularly during elections, as "sacrosanct" would oppose any limitations at all on the abilities of nonregistered participants to incur expenses to advertise their views. Not only are the objectives of fairness and equity deemed secondary, but many who support unfettered speech argue that fairness is obtained, not through limitations, but by the absence of them.

The electoral process, by analogy, becomes an electoral marketplace in which competition for voters' attention, among parties and candidates as well as interest groups, will ensure that the electorate is fully informed to cast a meaningful vote. Free speech, therefore, is equated with the right to spend money to advertise one's views. Regulations on groups' abilities to purchase advertising space or broadcast time undermine the opportunity to express the views of the organization. This view of freedom of expression is largely a negative one – freedom from interference – and rejects the claim that considerations such as access and opportunity are reasons for imposing limits.

The assumption that spending regulations impair freedom of expression is equally applicable to candidates and parties. According to this view, the current spending regulations on candidates and parties undermine the ability of election participants to make their policy positions known to electors and to distinguish their programs from those of their partisan rivals.

If spending limits for candidates and parties are retained and this asymmetry between candidates or parties and interest groups is, therefore, perceived as a problem, the solution is not to limit the speech of interest groups, but to remove the barriers facing candidates and parties.[45] The removal of all financial regulations governing interest groups would render irrelevant any attempts to distinguish between different forms of speech – for example, the advocacy of an issue as opposed to a candidate.

There are a number of criticisms of this approach, based largely on the American experience. American elections suggest that, if allowed, money assumes a highly prominent role, both in the direct spending of candidates and in the networks of support for candidates through PACs and independent expenditures. This raises concern about the possibility of corruption and undue influence, real or perceived, arising from candidates' dependence on wealthy contributors. Furthermore, the absence of spending regulations results in more expensive elections and prevents those of modest means or those without substantial PAC or interest group support from contesting elections in any meaningful way. A third criticism disputes the assumption that an unregulated economic environment enhances and facilitates free expression. The contrary argument is that, rather than being a free exchange of ideas, an unregulated environment becomes dominated and controlled by wealthy groups which monopolize the air waves and distort the electoral agenda.

2. Limits on Interest Groups Similar to Those on Parties and Candidates

This option rejects the unregulated environment assumed above, yet supports the proposition that, during elections, interest groups should not be treated in a qualitatively different manner than candidates and parties: parties and candidates should not be granted an exclusive right to the electoral stage, but must share that stage with other individuals or groups wanting to participate in a financial manner. Consequently, interest groups should be subject to the same kinds of financial regulations that apply to parties. They should also be entitled to the same range of expression. If parties are able to advertise positions in which they support their own candidates and oppose their foes, so too should interest groups.

The argument in favour of allowing interest groups to participate financially in elections asserts that independent expenditures allow for a more robust discussion of all the salient political concerns by addressing those issues for which parties are reluctant to assume policy positions. Furthermore, it is argued that parties' incapacity to represent the multitude of interests in Canada should not prevent those who do not identify with one of the parties from speaking out during elections.

Despite the claim that equal treatment for interest groups and candidates or parties (i.e., similar financial regulations and disclosure requirements) represents the fairest approach because it does not discriminate against either candidates, parties, individuals or interest groups, this view fails to address the distinctions between parties and interest groups in terms of the roles they perform and in their respective abilities to proliferate. Because parties, not interest groups, provide the main bridge between state action and electors' preferences, it is conceptually misleading to suggest that each is one of a number of different election participants, equally entitled to the same opportunities and obliged to face the same responsibilities. The fact that parties must appeal to a broad range of values and policy preferences and must reconcile conflicting regional and national tensions differentiates them from special interest groups which, by definition, are more narrowly conceived. There is the potential for an infinite number of issues around which individuals or groups can organize. Further, the suggestion that parties and interest groups should be treated as similar entities for the purpose of electoral regulations does not duly consider the impact of interest groups, through sheer numbers, on the political agenda. It does not consider, for example, that more than one group may promote a similar issue. In such an event, any attempt to ensure equity among all election participants (interest groups, candidates and parties) would be negated if interest groups were able to coordinate their activities (or proliferate for those purposes) to enhance the financial resources available to them.

The 1988 federal election provides a clear example of how the benefits of interest group advertising disproportionately favoured one party. If there had been spending limits on the amount each group could spend to promote free trade, there would likely have been little difference in the amount actually spent. The principal coalition of organizations favouring free trade (Canadian Alliance for Trade and Job Opportunities) could have spent as much money as it did, as long as the expenditures came from the various members of the Alliance.

In addition to maintaining meaningful spending limits on how much interest groups could spend to promote issues or candidates, there are a number of other enforcement problems which will be discussed in the third option.

3. Limits on Interest Groups Consistent with Their Role as Secondary Participants

A third option assesses freedom of expression from the perspective of the role parties perform and the electoral conditions that facilitate a healthy and vigorous competition between parties and candidates. While the abilities of individuals and organizations to financially promote their opinions is recognized as an important objective, the requirements of a free and equitable election process require that all financial activities during elections be regulated. Just as there are spending regulations for candidates and parties, and therefore some limits on their abilities to advertise their policy positions, so too should there be limits on interest groups and individuals to incur independent expenditures during elections. Unlike the second option, however, this approach rejects the assumption that interest groups and parties should be treated equally. Parties, from this perspective, are the primary election participants, whereas interest groups are secondary.

Freedom of expression must coexist with the principles of fairness and equity. There is a tension between these values. An interpretation of freedom of expression similar to that in the first option – freedom from interference – would make it difficult to ensure that there is equity or fair play in elections.

Promotion and Opposition of Candidates and Parties

It is difficult to conceive how the integrity of spending limits for candidates and parties can be preserved if interest groups are permitted to incur significant expenses to promote or oppose registered participants. The principal concern is the relatively modest spending ceilings for candidates at the local level. Any substantial spending by one or more interest groups could greatly disadvantage any candidate. While it might be argued that our parliamentary system of cabinet government and the Canadian practice of strict party discipline provide less incentive for interest groups to target candidates at the local level than in the United States, this does not mean that candidates are not vulnerable. The desire of many ideological groups to oppose candidates of a different policy persuasion or to take aim at candidates in swing or "soft" ridings makes candidates particularly susceptible to concentrated campaigns by interest groups.

These campaigns have even more potential to undermine fairness and equity when aimed at parties. The very reasons that may shield candidates from interest group activities – the fact that interest groups have difficulty influencing candidates' votes because of cabinet government and party discipline – make parties, as national entities, attractive to interest groups. If candidates are not promoted or opposed by interest groups because of their lack of influence on the policy of their party, the viable option for interest groups is to focus on the national level and influence the national policy agenda of government. Equity and fairness may be undermined, however, because it cannot be assumed that interest group support or opposition will have a similar effect for each party.

While one way of minimizing the extent to which independent expenditures undermine fairness and equity is to establish local or national limits on the amount of interest group advertising, there are a number of reasons why this is not viable. The first is the possibility that more than one group would target the same candidate or party, resulting in that recipient having received more publicity to promote a policy position favourable to his or her platform. The 1988 election provides a clear example of how a number of like-minded corporations and individuals coordinated their spending to maximize their advertising effort, the benefits of which disproportionately accrued to the Conservative party. Further, if the advertisement is negative or the message is misrepresented, the affected candidate and party may be financially constrained (because of spending limits) to dispute the advertised message.

While aggregate limits for individual contributions to interest groups' electoral advertisements would make it considerably more difficult for interest groups to proliferate, this remedy raises more problems than it would solve. For example, two of the difficulties that American enforcement officials face are the problem of individuals signing their names in different ways (for example, John H. Smith, J.H. Smith, J. Harry Smith), and corporations and unions giving money to employees or members to contribute. Effective enforcement of contribution limits would be even more problematic for Canada. While the American system has a relatively high aggregate individual contribution limit ($25 000 per year), the comparatively modest nature of spending limits for Canadian candidates and parties would require a much lower contribution limit. Unlike the American system, which does not rely on enforcement of individual violations to maintain the integrity of the system (most of the enforcement is directed at PACs rather than individual contributions), the dynamics of election spending in Canada would presume rigorous enforcement at the individual level. A second problem is the inevitable Charter problem of imposing contribution limits on some election participants, but not on others. If there were no contribution limits for candidates and parties (the primary election participants), it would be extremely difficult to justify contribution limits for interest groups.

A different enforcement problem is the question of whether the regulatory apparatus of the state should be applied to interest groups. Unlike the United States where the frequency of elections means that campaigning or fund raising never ends (and in which the structure of PACs was a direct response to the regulatory regime enacted in the 1970s), there are difficulties with importing disclosure rules for interest groups to Canada. Unlike PACs, Canadian interest groups operate in non-election environments. To the extent that elections occur on average every three or four years, the questions arise: How would disclosure requirements for elections impair or affect the other activities of the organization? Does the state have a legitimate role in monitoring the activities of interest groups which, other than during this brief period of election activity, may not be involved in electoral or partisan politics?

In light of the enforcement difficulties of regulating interest group expenditures, it is difficult to contemplate any significant opportunity for interest groups to promote or oppose candidates directly without irreparably undermining the principles of fairness and equity between registered participants.

Promotion of Issues

Having argued that fairness and equity for registered participants cannot be maintained if interest groups are permitted significant opportunities to advertise positions that directly promote or oppose candidates or parties, it is important to consider whether the advocacy of issues similarly undermines these principles. Even if a workable definition can be arrived at to distinguish partisan advocacy from the promotion of issues, many of the same concerns discussed in the context of promoting parties and candidates, such as multiplication of interest groups advancing a similar cause and enforcement difficulties, are relevant.

The likelihood that individuals and interest groups will tacitly or explicitly coordinate their efforts to promote a particular issue reinforces concerns that there is considerable potential for candidates and parties to be placed at a financial disadvantage. The 1988 experience, in which dozens of corporations mobilized financial support in the last two weeks of the election and spent an amount equal to more than three-quarters of all PC party election advertising revenues, shows the ease with which single organizations can proliferate and compound the significance of their advertising activities. The fact that the Conservative party received the benefit of an additional $3.6 million promoting the issue central to its platform suggests that even when primarily confined to the level of issue promotion as opposed to partisan advocacy, interest group advertisements can significantly undermine the principles of fairness and equity. Furthermore, the analysis of interest group election expenditures in 1988 suggests that, even though the vast majority of these advertisements did not specify the name of a candidate or party, advertisements in the last week of the campaign may have been responsible for a modest swing in voters' intentions.

The issue of interest group advertisements is relevant for all political parties and candidates. No political party is immune from the effects of interest groups trying to influence the election agenda. While the federal Conservative party benefited from the free trade advertising in the 1988 election, there is no reason to presume that it has an inherent advantage in this realm over other parties. Consider, for example, that if an election were called in the near future, a likely issue for interest group advertisements would be whether Canada should continue with or abandon the Goods and Services Tax. Even if these advertisements did not specifically identify the relevant parties by name, the fact that only one party favours the tax could result in these advertisements having the effect of directly promoting or opposing the Conservative party.

While it may be argued that the 1988 election was an exception in terms of interest group involvement, resulting from the importance of the free trade issue, there is no reason to assume that the experience with interest group advertising is peculiar to the free trade debate. Interest groups have not been significant election participants in Canada because the law since 1974 has prevented them from doing so. But the suggestion by a number of groups such as the National Citizens' Coalition and Campaign Life that elections are particularly critical times for them to advertise their policy views, and the fact that corporate groups have realized how quickly and effectively they can mobilize financial support on business-related issues during an election, suggest that the 1988 experience may well be part of a new trend in elections, rather than a sole occurrence. This conclusion is reinforced by the 1990 Ontario election experience where interest groups incurred significant expenditures independent of candidates and parties.

So far in this study it has been argued that any significant opportunity for interest groups to advertise policy or partisan positions at the local or national level will undermine the principles of fairness and equity. Problems enforcing the limits on either contributions to interest groups for election purposes or the amount of advertising that can be directed at any one candidate, party or issue invite more questions than answers.

While interest group expenditures undermine fairness and equity in the regulatory regime as it is currently defined, these expenditures would pose even greater problems if election regulations were to adopt a more inclusive definition of election expenses. Although the current spending regulations are strictly enforced, a number of activities are excluded from the definition of election expenses (the most notable example is polling). If, in fact, the definition were revised to include polling, there would be strong incentive for interest groups (surreptitiously or coincidentally) to advertise positions, hire consultants, or commission polls to enhance the publicity given to a particular issue. The more inclusive the definition of election expenses, the more difficult it becomes to conceptualize significant opportunities for interest group election advertising that would not irreparably undermine the spirit and intent of the spending limits imposed on parties and candidates.

Are Less Restrictive Means than a Total Ban an Option?

In light of these conclusions, it is important to consider whether there is any way to allow interest groups or individuals financial expression. In the aftermath of the 1984 constitutional decision that the restrictions on interest groups' abilities to directly promote or oppose candidates or parties were unconstitutional, the Chief Electoral Officer himself suggested that a less restrictive means of limiting the expression of interest groups may be available.[46] What Jean-Marc Hamel contemplated was a ban on access to the mass media for anyone or any group other than candidates or parties and an extremely modest spending limit (between $100 and $200), which individuals or interest groups could spend on items such as brochures, leaflets or lawn signs (Hamel 1990).

While the remedy Hamel proposed was a response to the challenge presented by the Citizens' Coalition that expression must enable individuals or groups to link the promotion of issues to candidates and parties, the ban on all media advertising represents another serious Charter problem. The fact that interest groups are not merely limited but prohibited from reliance on the media raises problems in assuring the Court that this represents the least restrictive means available.

While the ban on media advertising may have been difficult to justify under section 1 of the Charter, Hamel's approach provides a useful model for regulating interest groups during elections. The idea that individuals or interest groups should be able to spend a modest amount of money on any form of advertising (both issue and partisan advocacy) would satisfy arguments that meaningful expression must encompass the ability both to promote issues and to link this promotion to candidates and parties.

It is highly probable that any spending limit for interest groups would be subject to a Charter challenge for violating freedom of expression. While this option would limit expression, particularly if expression is equated with the right to spend money, limits would not prevent individuals and groups from advertising positions on issues, candidates or parties. What the spending limits would in effect prevent is significant use of the commercial media during the election period to advertise positions to a larger audience. Alternatives to media-centred advertising could be employed, such as the printing and circulation of pamphlets or leaflets, the purchase and distribution of pins, the use of lawn signs and similar inexpensive forms of communication. This approach need not preclude interest groups from gaining access to television. Two studies discussing how to reconcile fairness with interest group behaviour suggest that public or community television could be made available to interest groups during elections. One suggestion calls for the use of "free time" broadcasts on the parliamentary television channel during the election so that interest groups can present their views on the election. This time could be allocated by the Broadcasting Arbitrator. It is argued that this approach would not only address the need to ensure fairness among candidates and parties, but would contribute to an informed electorate (Axworthy 1991). A different variation of this suggestion is to provide time on the CBC news channel (in which interest groups could purchase time) that would be allocated and subsidized by the government (Brock 1991). The justification for this approach is that it represents the best attempt to reconcile the tension between the competing values – freedom of expression on the one hand and equity and fairness on the other – and also it imposes as little restriction as possible on the electoral expression of interest groups and individuals while maintaining the integrity of candidate or party spending limits.

While this option still has the potential to undermine spending limits, particularly for local candidates, legislation could be designed to preclude groups from coordinating their activities in a way that would undermine the intent of the limitations. If, for example, the legislation explicitly prevented interest groups or individuals from spending more than a prescribed amount (in the range, perhaps, of $500 to $1 000) to directly or indirectly promote or oppose candidates or parties and required as well that the name of the sponsor be clearly identified in any material or advertisement, and prevented the coordination of expenses with any other individual or organization, many of the enforcement and proliferation problems discussed earlier could be avoided, or at least minimized. For instance, significant commercial television advertising and direct mail, newspaper, radio or magazine advertisements would likely exceed the allowable spending; the violation of the regulation, therefore, would be readily apparent. Enforcement of violations would also rely on the receipt of complaints. In either case, a viable way of preventing these expenditures from having any deeper impact on the election would be to seek an injunction against further advertising. In that case the publicity arising from the fact that a group or individual had contravened the law would significantly offset any advantages incurred to the candidate or party being promoted during the advertisement. Because the system would be based on modest spending limits, there would be no need for disclosure which imposes additional restrictions on individuals or groups.

This option further contemplates a prohibition on interest group advertising on the day before the poll and the election day itself, as is the situation for candidates and parties. It will be remembered from the discussion of Campaign Life that some of the most negative advertising was distributed on the eve of the 1988 election when candidates were legally incapable of responding. Commission research identified 12 newspaper advertisements by interest groups during the ban at the end of the campaign. A requirement that interest groups respect the ban at the start of elections was also suggested in a number of presentations to this Commission. There were, in fact, 30 such newspaper advertisements by interest groups that were identified during this period of the 1988 election. It may be argued, however, that in light of the modest allowable spending limits contemplated for individuals and interest groups, a ban on independent advertising expenditures during the first part of the election is not crucial because candidates and parties would have plenty of time to respond to allegations.

One advantage of this approach is that, like Hamel's proposed model, it does not make what could be considered an artificial distinction between candidate and issue advocacy. There would be no restrictions on how or where groups or individuals advertise as long as they do not exceed the spending limit; do not coordinate advertisements with any other individual or group; do not advertise during the election period ban that applies to candidates and parties; and identify the name of the sponsor.

This approach addresses the concern raised by Mr. Justice Medhurst in the *National Citizens' Coalition* case – that the legislation should not prevent an individual from spending a few dollars to photocopy a pamphlet exhorting the reader to vote in a particular way (Tarte 1990). Although small scale activities of this kind do not pose a serious threat to the spending limits for candidates and parties, under the 1983 legislation they were formally prohibited. Even though prosecutorial discretion would likely have prevented litigating these marginal abuses, the Supreme Court has made it clear that prosecutorial discretion is an inadequate substitute for a more carefully and narrowly defined law (*Smith* 1987).

The fact that organizations would not be treated differently than individuals (they would be subject to the same spending limits) and that individuals and/or organizations could not coordinate their spending allotments would mean that the bulk of the spending would be incurred by individuals. The requirement that each advertisement or promotional material would have to designate the name of the particular sponsor would mean that the overwhelming majority of materials would not bear an organization's name but would in fact identify the particular individual sponsor. This would greatly alleviate the impact on candidates' or parties' spending limits of concentrated campaigns by a particular organization, via coordination of spending by individual members.

While it is highly probable that if enacted, interest groups, corporations and unions would respond to this approach by exhorting members to act in a particular way during elections, such activity is not, and should not be seen as, a violation of the fairness and equity principle. While there is little to prevent interest groups from encouraging members to spend their allowable limit to advertise a policy position, any attempt to limit the communication within organizations during elections would likely be challenged as an unreasonable limit on freedom of association. It could be difficult to argue that a limit on this form of communication is necessary to ensure the integrity of candidate and party spending limits. However, this principle and any law upon which it was based would be violated if groups were to spend in excess of their legal limit to communicate with those outside their organizations. The spending limits would be triggered by any commercial advertisement during the election period, aimed at those beyond the regular membership, which promoted a policy position relating to any election issue, candidate or party.

Although the modest spending limits would essentially preclude organizations from significant advertising activity during elections, it might not discourage them from participating on an individual member basis. This is philosophically defensible. Freedom of expression is largely an individual right. While there has been an extension of this right to organizations (*Ford* 1988; *Irwin Toy* 1989), the genesis of freedom of expression in liberal democracies, particularly in an electoral context, is the opportunity for individual voters to assess and criticize those who hold or seek office. If interest groups or organizations want to participate in elections in a more substantive way, they have the option of doing so by registering as a political party and fielding candidates.

4. Ban on All Expenses during Elections by Nonregistered Participants

The most effective way of ensuring the integrity of spending limits for candidates and parties would be to ban all election expenses by those other than registered candidates and parties. While it is an improvement on the third option from an enforcement perspective, there are still a number of difficulties with this approach. The most serious is the constitutional difficulty of demonstrating under section 1 of the Charter that there is no way of allowing interest groups or individuals to spend money to promote their policy views while ensuring that the electoral process is fair and equitable for registered participants.

While it would be a mistake to predict what the Supreme Court's response to this option would be, one can suggest with some certainty that the Court would ask the question: Are there less restrictive means available? Mr. Justice Medhurst's disapproval of the fact in the *Coalition* case that an individual could not legally spend a few dollars to distribute home-made pamphlets represents a serious, and perhaps impossible, hurdle to be overcome by this approach. It is hard to conceive how this modest example of free speech irreparably harms the spending limits for candidates and parties.

While it is questionable whether this option would survive a Charter challenge, there is another constitutional remedy. The legislative override in section 33 provides governments with a five-year, renewable exemption from the applicability of most of the provisions in the Charter. While there is no doubt about the constitutionality of this provision, there is considerable question about the political ramifications resulting from its use. Since the entrenchment of fundamental rights and freedoms in the Charter in 1982, the language of rights has so captured the public's imagination that enacting the legislative override has virtually become politically impossible. The overwhelming belief that governments should not deliberately pursue policies that are in direct conflict with protected rights has made it difficult for governments to consider openly the use of the override.

The use of the override is particularly unpopular outside Quebec. In 1988 Premier Bourassa's reliance on section 33 to protect his government's new commercial sign law from a potential Charter challenge immediately prompted calls for a constitutional amendment to remove the override and demands that the federal government never use it. The belief that rights are only meaningful if politicians cannot tamper with them has been fuelled, particularly at the popular level, by continued attacks on the override by high-ranking public officials. Prime Minister Mulroney, for instance, suggested that the constitutional amendments proclaimed in 1982 are virtually worthless because, aside from dividing the nation, they fail to protect Canadians' rights: "A Constitution that does not protect the inalienable and imprescriptible individual rights of individual Canadians is not worth the paper that it is written on" (*Ottawa Citizen* 7 April 1989, A1–2).

While parties are the primary participants in election debates, this does not mean they should be immune from modest attempts to influence or contribute to the election agenda. Legislation which, at its most extreme, prevents an individual from handing out home-made leaflets on the street, or promoting or opposing a particular candidate or party is, intuitively and philosophically, incompatible with a commitment to free expression. While it is debatable whether adequate expression depends on large resources to advertise views and to reach out to a broad regional or national audience, it does mean more than the formal recognition of the right to speak. Some ability to communicate with others is required. Consequently, it is important that individuals or groups have, at the very least, some opportunity to incur modest expenses to communicate with each other for the purpose of political discourse.

It may be argued that a prohibition on interest group advertising is reasonable because it is extremely short in duration. But this argument has a serious shortcoming. It is precisely *during* the election period when the ability to speak out and criticize government and those who seek office is most important.

CONCLUSIONS

The issue of whether interest groups should be able to participate financially during elections has generated considerable debate, attracting more than 100 intervenors before this Royal Commission – more than on any issue other than campaign and party finance. These intervenors and others who submitted briefs to the Commission made suggestions for dealing with interest groups that ranged from no regulations at all on interest groups to no avenues for financial participation.

Reflected in the various suggestions are conceptually different views of two issues: the question of which values deserve primacy during elections (freedom of expression or fairness and equity), and the nexus between interest groups and parties during elections.

One view, greatly influenced by the Charter, posits that freedom of expression is the most important value during elections and should not be limited for any reason. Freedom of expression is essentially interpreted as a negative liberty – freedom from interference – and is equated with the ability to spend money. Limits on advertising, therefore, limit the effectiveness of interest groups and individuals to address the range of issues they wish to promote. Furthermore, restrictions on individuals and interest groups to advertise policy positions detract from the ability of the electorate to make informed voting decisions.

The views that freedom of expression requires unlimited opportunities to advertise positions or issues and that unregulated advertising represents the best way of educating voters so they can make informed electoral decisions have significant implications for political parties and candidates. Parties, from this perspective, are among a number of election participants and should not be given preferential treatment at the expense of freedom of expression.

In light of the view that parties ought to be treated like any other interested group, there is little currency to the argument that because unregulated interest group election spending is in conflict with spending limits for parties and candidates, this asymmetry should be addressed by regulating interest groups. The extension of the argument that freedom of expression is achieved by eliminating regulations is to remove the spending limits for all election participants, including candidates and parties.

The second perspective rejects the assumption that parties should be considered as just one of a number of election participants. Given that parties provide the bridge between state actions and the interests of society, parties and candidates are seen as the principal election participants, while interest groups and nonregistered individuals are secondary participants.

Furthermore, as a result of 1974 legislative reforms, the principles of fairness and equity have emerged as basic assumptions of how elections should be conducted. The belief that money should not unduly influence the election process and that registered participants should compete on a relatively equitable footing is reflected in the regulations that limit spending by candidates and parties, and disclosure laws. Consequently, this approach rejects the assumption that freedom of speech is equated with the right to spend money. Just as the principles of fairness and equity have primacy over the right of candidates and parties to spend money without limit during elections in order to advertise their positions, so these same principles should also have primacy over the right of interest groups and individuals to advertise their positions.

While this perspective does not suggest that interest groups or individuals cannot exercise some degree of free speech during elections, it approaches the issue of interest group election participation from the perspective of maintaining fairness and equity in the financial regulatory regime. Difficulties in maintaining meaningful distinctions between different forms of speech (issue versus partisan advocacy), the inevitable proliferation of groups around specific issues and the enforcement difficulties that render spending limits meaningless, lead to the conclusion that independent expenditures have to be tightly controlled.

Neither of the different views of the nexus between interest groups and candidates or parties during elections is without problems. The difficulty with the first assumption is that the equation of parties with other groups competing for public attention during elections does not give due consideration to the importance of parties in choosing government. The second view which sees candidates and parties as the primary, although not necessarily exclusive, election participants does not adequately address the considerable gap between the role parties are expected to serve and the role they in fact are assuming. This shortcoming is reflected in the fact that interest groups are gaining a significant profile on the electoral stage.

While neither conception is without difficulties, a central premise of this study has been that the preferred view is that parties are the primary election participants. Whatever shortcomings exist between the roles parties are expected to fill and public perceptions of their performance, parties remain the most effective instruments of ordering our election preferences and of choosing government – short of institutional reforms encompassing how we translate our electoral choices into elected representatives and, in turn, governments. A more fragmented system, in which interest groups increasingly portray election choices as specific responses to particular policy positions, will undermine the capacity of parties to generate the kind of consensus that is increasingly more difficult and, consequently more necessary, for governing.

While this does not preclude individuals or interest groups from having a role during elections to evaluate and criticize those who seek public office, there is a need to place limits on these opportunities. This need arises not only from the assumption that parties are the principal election participants, but also because the central values of the election process – fairness and equity – presume regulations will limit the impact of money during elections. The operating requirements of these values mean that all election spending, which undermines the capacity of registered participants to present themselves during elections in a fair manner and on an equitable basis, be regulated. Given the potential, indeed likelihood, that interest groups will proliferate around particular election issues, and the almost insurmountable difficulties in ensuring that their advertising campaigns do not nullify the intent of candidate or party spending limits, the preferred approach to regulating interest group election involvement is the third option.

This would mean that individuals or interest groups could advertise positions on issues, candidates and parties (although without adopting measures to provide access to commercial television, groups could at best afford only nominal advertisements on commercial television). But these advertisements could not be coordinated with any other individual or interest group. While the modest spending limit would preclude those who are not registered as candidates and parties from relying on the mass media to influence the election agenda, it would not preclude them from discussing issues with members or other interested individuals, or prevent them from distributing materials that seek to influence voters' intentions. Problems of enforcing the larger advertising campaigns by interest groups or individuals would be so significant that they would call into question the purpose and objectives of the candidate or party spending limits. There would also be other restraints on interest groups resulting from the likely requirements for registration and disclosure.

Given that a central role of parties is to provide the means by which Canadians' interests and values are ordered, defined and translated into policy, this study has argued that the policy decision on the issue of interest group election involvement should be based on the requirements of a fair and equitable election system for candidates and parties, rather than the ability of interest groups to use the election stage to advance their own organizational or ideological objectives.

While attempts to reconcile conflicting values and principles inevitably generate criticism, the preferred option represents a balanced approach to ensuring meaningful expression of interest groups and individuals who choose not to associate with parties, while at the same time maintaining the cornerstone values of the Canadian election process – fairness and equity. Furthermore, it is the option that best achieves this with the minimum impairment of expression possible – a necessary objective in light of the Charter and a desirable accomplishment in itself.

ABBREVIATIONS

All E.R.	All England Law Reports
Alta. L.R. (2d)	Alberta Law Reports, Second Series
Alta. Q.B.	Alberta Queen's Bench
am.	amended
c.	chapter
cir.	circuit
Co. Ct.	County Court
C.R. (4th)	Criminal Reports, Fourth Series

C.S.P.	Recueils de jurisprudence, Cour des sessions de la paix (Que.)
en.	enacted
F.2d	Federal Reporter, Second Series
K.B.	King's Bench Division
O.R. (2d)	Ontario Reports, Second Series
Pub. L.	Public Law (U.S.)
R.	Regina
R.S.C.	Revised Statutes of Canada
R.S.N.S.	Revised Statutes of Nova Scotia
R.S.Q.	Revised Statutes of Quebec
R.S.S.	Revised Statutes of Saskatchewan
s(s).	section(s)
S.C.	Statutes of Canada
S.C.C.	Supreme Court of Canada
S.C.R.	Supreme Court Reports
U.S.	United States Supreme Court Reports
W.W.R.	Western Weekly Reports

NOTES

This study was completed 29 April 1991.

I would like to thank Don Padget and Victor Manuel Sanchez-Velarde for coding the interest group election advertising under the supervision of Jean Crête and with analysis by Richard Johnston. I would also like to acknowledge the useful research by Don Padget on interest group participation in the 1988 federal and 1990 Ontario elections. I am grateful to Leslie Seidle for the suggestions he made on earlier versions of this study, as well as the comments of two anonymous reviewers.

1. Although the term "third parties" is widely used in the Canadian literature to describe nonregistered participants, it creates confusion because the term also has another meaning (the description of minor political parties). Because of this confusion and to avoid any pejorative implications of the term, nonregistered participants will generally be referred to as interest groups.

2. While not formerly provided for in the *Constitution Act, 1867*, the *Canada Elections Act*, s. 190(1)(*a*) specifies that the candidate receiving the most votes in any constituency is the elected candidate.

3. *Irwin Toy Ltd. v. Quebec (Attorney General)* (1989, 976–77). Although the Court found it unnecessary to delineate precisely when and on what basis a form of expression falls outside the sphere of protection, it did articulate three principles, and suggested that expression should reflect at least one if it is to be protected: 1) expression which seeks and attains the truth; 2) expression which fosters and encourages participation in social and political decision making; and 3) expression which cultivates a diversity in forms of individual self-fulfilment and human flourishing in a tolerant, welcoming environment.

4. The Barbeau Committee was established after the federal government announced in the Throne Speech of 18 Feb. 1964 its intention to establish a committee of inquiry " to advise on the best practicable way to set enforceable limits to expenditures in election campaigns."

5. In defending the legislation, the federal government produced the following evidence of mischief: an advertisement by the Jewish Joint Public Relations Committee in the Kitchener–Waterloo riding on the eve of the 1980 election attacking a federal Liberal candidate at a time when no response was permitted; a threat by the International Fund for Animal Welfare to spend $3 000 000 in Metropolitan Toronto during an upcoming election to defeat Liberal candidates who were not supportive of the organization's policy to end the Canadian seal hunt; advertisements published by the National Citizens' Coalition costing $150 000 during the 1979 general election and $160 000 in the 1980 election, many of them opposed to registered candidates; and billboards, signs and flyers sponsored by the Coalition opposing Jim Coutts, Liberal candidate in the Toronto riding of Spadina during the 1981 by-election (Canada, Attorney General 1984, Second Submission, 2–5).

6. The government could have argued that interest groups are free to promote candidates and parties financially provided that they coordinate these activities with the official campaign and are subject, therefore, to spending limits.

7. For a discussion on the policy reasons for the decisions not to appeal or introduce new legislation, see Hiebert (1989–90).

8. George Allen, Commissioner of Canada Elections, decided to uphold the previous policy decision of Gorman not to enforce the spending regulations: interview 24 March 1988.

9. The newspapers analysed for interest group advertisements were the following: Halifax *Chronicle-Herald,* St. John's *Telegram,* Saint John *Telegraph-Journal,* Montreal *La Presse,* Montreal *Le Devoir,* Quebec City *Le Soleil,* Montreal *Gazette,* Toronto *Star,* Toronto *Globe and Mail,* Ottawa *Le Droit, Winnipeg Free Press,* Regina *Leader Post, Edmonton Journal,* and Vancouver *Sun.*

10. The exception is the television advertising by Le Regroupement pour le libre-échange, which is included in the official figures provided by the Canadian Alliance for Trade and Job Opportunities.

11. Richard Johnston, Memo to the Commission. Subsequent analysis suggests the impact of interest group advertisement on voters' intent may have been even higher. See Johnston et al. (1991).

12. Figure obtained in Audited Statement of the Canadian Alliance for Trade and Job Opportunities, Statement of Receipts and Disbursements, Year End 31 March 1989. This figure includes the expenditures of Le Regroupement pour le libre-échange.

13. Analysis of four newspapers in Quebec during the election indicates that Le Regroupement pour le libre-échange spent $71 000. In addition to the newspaper advertisements, approximately $29 000 was spent on television advertisements.

14. Figure obtained from Audited Statement of the Canadian Alliance for Trade and Job Opportunities (1989). The actual expenditure on advertising from 23 April 1987 to 31 March 1988 was $1 736 247. In addition the Alliance paid $650 000 in consulting fees, close to $150 000 in professional fees, and $180 000 in polling research. Total expenditures in that year were $2 861 820, while contributions were $2 968 169.

15. Ibid., 75. The Alliance launched an employee program with the purpose of encouraging employers to inform and educate their employees as to how the Free Trade Agreement would "benefit them, their company and community." The Alliance's involvement in the employee campaigns consisted of providing a benefits summary, case histories and related materials to implement the program.

16. The figure of $5.25 million relates to the two-year period between the Alliance's inception in the spring of 1987 until March 1989; the latter two expenditures were incurred in the fiscal year 1988 and, while directly related to the free trade issue, were not confined exclusively to the electoral period.

17. The idea for the comic book arose after a number of coalitions opposed to free trade from across the country made requests for information on the issue of free trade which was accessible and understandable to readers (Bleyer 1990). The work behind the comic book preceded the election call although the release occurred early in the campaign in the second week of October.

18. Salutin (1989, 260) suggests 40 percent of the cost of the comic book was raised by labour.

19. (Bleyer 1990). The Network was approached by *Maclean's* magazine which attempted to sell space to the organization in a final free trade issue shortly before voting day. The organization declined, because of a shortage of

cash, and was given a complimentary two-page advertisement in the magazine, which contained a five-page advertisement paid for by the Alliance. There is some question whether, in fact, the space was provided free of charge, or was subsidized. Correspondence with Maclean Hunter suggests that the advertisement was sold for $4 259.50, reduced from the normal market rate of $24 699.50. The value of this advertisement was not included in the estimated expenditures for the Pro-Canada Network.

20. Somerville suggests that the decision to target Broadbent was made before the election was called because the NDP was particularly high in the polls and the Coalition wanted to undermine any possibility of improved NDP electoral success.

21. Campaign Life often circulates a questionnaire that asks candidates to state their position on the issue of choice regarding abortion. Hughes suggests this tactic is effective because candidates, thinking that they are responding to a pro-choice organization, are more candid about their position.

22. Among the more negative advertisements by Campaign Life during the election was a pamphlet distributed to Toronto area homes displaying Liberal or NDP signs. The brochures accused NDP incumbent Dan Heap and Liberal candidate Tony Ianno of supporting "legalized killing of children in the womb." On one side of the brochure, the following question was posed: "Guess who believes its okay for some children to go to the Dung Heap?" On the other side of the pamphlet, under a picture depicting an advanced fetus that had been grossly mutilated, the question was answered with Heap's name in large type. The pamphlet concluded by saying that support of either Heap or Ianno "is a vote to continue this human slaughter" (*Toronto Star*, 20 Nov. 1988). Hughes confirmed that the pamphlet was distributed by his organization.

23. In the skit a nurse, complaining that bed closings had required that a patient with gangrene be placed in a bed next to a man just out of surgery, stated: "Of course, we wash up after each patient, but you never know how those little organisms can travel."

24. The NCC spent an estimated $15 000 in the election.

25. The exceptions include the following: the cost of publishing news articles or broadcasting public affairs or news programs, provided that they are published without payment or reward; the cost of producing, promoting and distributing a book that was planned for publication independent of the election call; the cost of broadcasting and a number of activities relating directly to the candidate selection process and candidate campaign activities. For a complete list of exemptions, see Quebec *Election Act*, s. 404.

26. Excluded from the list of prohibited expenses are editorials in newspapers or other periodicals, radio or television news programs or commentaries.

27. It is arguable that the above reference means only that groups cannot run front or parallel campaigns to support or oppose a particular candidate as a way of deliberately circumventing the spending limits. Saskatchewan Chief Electoral Officer Keith Lampard indicates that while provincial justice officials interpret the good faith defence in a narrower manner (as the ability to promote issues), federal justice officials suggest that the clause has broader implications and would allow groups or individuals to identify candidate or party names in advertisements.

28. Among the advertisements were: a mock ballot with the label "Instructions to Vote" and an X beside the name of an NDP candidate; a pamphlet urging voters to vote for a particular Conservative candidate, stating that Liberal and NDP candidates supported the "killing of children by abortion" and a pamphlet criticizing cuts in programs and funding for battered women and the mentally and physically disabled, urging readers to "stand with us in saying 'NO MORE!' "

29. There is an important distinction in the composition of PACs: non-connected and connected PACs. Connected PACs are able to pay administrative, start-up and solicitation costs out of general treasury funds, but can only solicit members, in the case of unions, or shareholders and administrative personnel, in the case of corporations. Non-connected PACs can solicit anyone but all funding must come from these solicitations rather than general revenues.

30. There has been a ban on direct corporate contributions to the election of federal officials dating back to the Tillman Act of 1907. The impetus for the legislation was concern that the concentration of newly acquired industrial capital in the post–Civil War period was being used to corrupt the political process. When it became apparent that disclosure laws were unsuccessful in halting corruption, reformers pushed for a complete ban on corporation contributions to any political committee or for any political purpose. The prohibition was extended to labour unions in 1943. For good discussions on the historical origins of PAC regulations, see Matasar (1986) and Mutch (1988).

31. Legislation in 1971 allowed unions and corporations to use treasury funds to establish and operate PACs. Labour officials lobbied for legislation allowing unions and corporations to establish and operate PACs after a union was indicted in 1968 for violating the prohibition on union political contributions (*Pipefitters* 1972). This called into question the longstanding practice of unions using general treasury funds for political purposes. Organized labour included corporations in their lobbying efforts to secure greater support for the legislation. At the time, corporate PACs were not perceived by organized labour as a strong threat because of an existing law which precluded firms that were doing contract work for the government (many of the nation's largest corporations) from contributing directly or indirectly to federal election campaigns. See Alexander (1984) and Mutch (1988).

32. What is ironic about this change is that it was labour which actually lobbied to have the prohibition lifted. Having secured government contracts to train workers, some labour unions became concerned that their ability to maintain PACs might be threatened unless the law was changed. The 1974 amendments not only addressed labour's concerns but also permitted corporations with large defence and other contracts to use corporate funds to establish and administer their PACs. Furthermore, the enactment of an individual contribution limit of $1 000, which emphasized the value of a large number of small contributions, provided corporations with the motivation to establish PACs.

33. The requirements for the second-tier contribution limits are that the political committee must be registered with the FEC for at least six months, receive contributions from more than 50 persons, and contribute to at least five candidates for federal office. The vast majority of PACs qualify as a multi-candidate committee and are subject to the following limits: $5 000 to any candidate for federal office per election; $15 000 to the national committee of a political party; and $5 000 to any other political committee.

34. Quoted from *New York Times Co. v. Sullivan* 376 U.S. 254 at 269 (1963), quoting *Associated Press v. United States* 326 U.S. 1 at 20 (1945).

35. The limits applied to expenditures made by an authorized committee of the candidate or any other agent of the candidate as well as any expenditure by any other person that is "authorized or requested" by the candidate or his agent. The ceilings, which were based on the voting age population, set a maximum limit of $70 000 for campaigns for the House of Representatives, $150 000 for elections to the Senate, and $20 000 000 for the presidency election. These figures did not include contesting primaries or nominations.

36. The fact that many PACs tend to be associated with a particular business, industry or society group means that the voting records of individual members to the House of Representatives and the nature of the states or districts they represent result in PACs being more inclined to support candidates for the House of Representatives than for the Senate.

37. The other side of this argument is that PACs are largely responsible for the decline of political parties. By providing substantial amounts of campaign moneys for candidates, they decrease candidates' reliance on political parties. A related criticism is that PACs and interest groups have increasingly assumed the role of promoting particular interests at the expense of the parties' role in adjudicating among competing interests or values (Drew 1982, 68–71; Alexander 1984, 100).

38. In the Court's view, a small issue-based group should not be subject to the kinds of regulations facing large economic corporations because the requirement for segregated funds would result in organizational and financial hardship that would burden freedom of expression. The Court articulated

three characteristics that distinguish voluntary, idea-based political associations from business organizations. The former cannot be required to segregate funds for political expenditures, unlike business organizations. To be exempt from the regulations governing economic PACs, an organization must have the following characteristics: it must have been created for the purpose of promoting political ideas; there must be no shareholders or other affiliated persons who would have a claim on its assets or earnings; and the organization must not accept contributions from business corporations or labour unions.

39. The following information is required: the reporting person's name, mailing address, occupation and the name of the employer; the identification of the person to whom the expenditure was made; the amount, date and purpose of each expenditure; a statement indicating whether the expenditure was in support of or in opposition to a candidate, together with the candidate's name and office sought; a notarized certification as to whether the expenditure was made in cooperation, consultation or concert with any candidate, authorized committee or agent; and the identification of each person who made a contribution of more than $200 to the person filing the report (United States 1990, 109.2).

40. Much of the criticism of the enforcement problems faced by the FEC focuses on the structure of the Commission, including its partisan composition, the weakness of the role of the chairperson, and budget limitations. In the view of one commentator: "The inability of the Commission to deal promptly with campaign finance abuses and seemingly, in the eyes of many observers, to be subject to partisan pressures, accurately reflects the intention of Congress to establish a weak agency responsive to the political wishes of the existing power base ... 'Congress designed the Commission to fail, building in the propensity for partisan deadlocks, insisting on the appointment of pliant Commissioners, and creating a morass of procedural defenses for suspected wrongdoers'" (Reiche 1990, 238). For more discussion of the FEC in terms of enforcement, see Gross (1989), and Magleby and Nelson (1990).

41. The law intended that the process for launching complaints be an easy one. Consequently, any interested individual can launch a complaint providing that he or she identify the name of the individual or organization that allegedly violated the regulations and specify the nature of the violation. The process is relatively informal. The statement need only be notarized and delivered to the Commission.

42. The legal difficulty is that corporations are not allowed to do indirectly what they cannot do directly. Just as corporations cannot directly promote candidates or parties, neither can employees acting on their behalf. Similarly, "arranged" employee PAC contributions, for the purpose of exceeding a corporation's legal contribution limit, are unlawful.

43. The National Citizen's Coalition is an exception.

44. More than 40 individuals wrote to the Commission on this subject.

45. This is the view of the National Citizens' Coalition. Somerville suggests that there is no legitimacy to any regulations that restrict the abilities of individuals or groups to spend whatever money they wish to advertise their views. If pressed on the question of the imbalance between spending limits for candidates and parties and the absence of restrictions for interest groups, Somerville responds that it is not his organization's fault that the system limits candidates or parties. In his view all spending regulations should be removed.

46. Chief Electoral Officer Jean-Marc Hamel did not outline how the legislation could better enable interest groups to express themselves during elections. He recommended only that the question be looked at "with a view to striking a proper balance between the adequate control of election expenses and the freedom of expression of Canadians." In his view, the solution could be found in the imposition "of certain restrictions on third parties not amounting to a total prohibition" (Canada, Elections Canada 1984, 24).

INTERVIEWS

Allen, George, Commissioner of Canada Elections, 24 Mar. 1988.

*Barry, Francine, Legal Department, Office of the Chief Electoral Officer of Quebec, 25 Sept. 1990.

Biersack, Robert, Federal Election Commission Chief Statistician, 16 Oct. 1990.

*Bleyer, Peter, Political Action Co-ordinator Pro-Canada Network, 30 Aug. 1990.

*Boivin, Natalie, TVA, 25 Oct. 1990.

Collins, Huguette, former administrative assistant to Joseph Gorman, Commissioner of Canada Elections, 16 Sept. 1987.

*Ferguson, Cherry, Nova Scotia Chief Electoral Officer, 25 Sept. 1990.

*Fordham, Art, Former Assistant Chief Electoral Officer of Nova Scotia, 25 Sept. 1990.

*Fraser, Jack, Chairperson, Manitoba Committee for Free Trade, 15 Oct. 1990.

*French, Larry, Ontario Secondary School Teachers' Federation Legislative Researcher, 3 Dec. 1990.

Hamel, Jean-Marc, former Chief Electoral Officer of Canada, 31 Nov. 1990.

*Harrison, Len, Canadian Auto Workers' Political Education Director, 6 Dec. 1990.

Hughes, James, National President Campaign Life Coalition, 6 Sept. 1990.

*Lampard, Keith, Saskatchewan Chief Electoral Officer, 15 Nov. 1990.

Lerner, Lois, FEC Associate General Counsel for Enforcement, 15 Oct. 1990.

*Nicholls, Gerry, National Citizens' Coalition, 7 Jan. 1991.

*Rhodes, Paul, Government Affairs Representative of the Ontario Medical Association, 4 Dec. 1990.

Somerville, David, National Citizens' Coalition, 6 Sept. 1990.

Tarte, Yvon, Legal Adviser to the Chief Electoral Officer of Canada, 5 Dec. 1990.

*Interviews conducted by Don Padget, Royal Commission Research Analyst.

REFERENCES

Adamany, David. 1980. "PACs and the Democratic Financing of Politics." *Arizona Law Review* 22:569–602.

Alexander, Herbert. 1984. *Financing Politics: Money, Elections and Political Reform*. 3d ed. Washington, DC: Congressional Quarterly Inc.

Associated Press v. United States 326 U.S. 1 (1945).

Axworthy, Thomas S. 1991. "Capital-Intensive Politics: Money, Media and Mores in the United States and Canada." In *Issues in Party and Election Finance in Canada*, ed. F. Leslie Seidle. Vol. 5 of the research studies of the Royal Commission on Electoral Reform and Party Financing. Ottawa and Toronto: RCERPF/Dundurn.

Boucher v. Centrale de l'enseignement du Québec, [1982] C.S.P. 1003.

Brock, Kathy L. 1991. "Fairness, Equity, and Rights." In *Political Ethics: A Canadian Perspective*, ed. Janet Hiebert. Vol. 12 of the research studies of the Royal Commission on Electoral Reform and Party Financing. Ottawa and Toronto: RCERPF/Dundurn.

Buckley v. Valeo 424 U.S. 1 (1976).

Butler, D.E., and R. Rose. 1960. *The British General Election of 1959*. London: Macmillan.

Canada. *An Act to Amend the Canada Elections Act (No. 3)*, S.C. 1980–81–82–83, c. 164, s. 2.

———. *Canada Elections Act*, R.S.C. 1970, c. 14 (1st Supp.), s. 70.1, en. 1973–74, c. 51, s. 12; am. 1980–81–82–83, c. 164, s. 14.

———. *Canada Elections Act*, R.S.C. 1985, c. E-2, s. 190.

———. *Canadian Charter of Rights and Freedoms*, ss. 2(b), 33, Part I of the *Constitution Act, 1982*, being Schedule B of the *Canada Act 1982* (U.K.), 1982, c. 11.

Canada. Attorney General. 1984. First and Second Submissions, *National Citizens' Coalition Inc. v. Canada (Attorney General)*. Ottawa.

Canada. Committee on Election Expenses. 1966. *Report*. Ottawa: Queen's Printer.

Canada. Elections Canada. 1979. *Statutory Report of the Chief Electoral Officer as per subsection 59(1) of the Canada Elections Act*. Ottawa: Minister of Supply and Services Canada.

———. 1980. *Statutory Report of the Chief Electoral Officer as per subsection 59(1) of the Canada Elections Act*. Ottawa: Minister of Supply and Services Canada.

———. 1983. *Statutory Report of the Chief Electoral Officer as per subsection 59(1) of the Canada Elections Act*. Ottawa: Minister of Supply and Services Canada.

———. 1984. *Statutory Report of the Chief Electoral Officer as per subsection 59(1) of the Canada Elections Act*. Ottawa: Minister of Supply and Services Canada.

———. 1988. *Report of the Chief Electoral Officer Respecting Election Finances, Thirty-Fourth General Election, 1988*. Ottawa: Minister of Supply and Services Canada.

Canada. House of Commons. 1983. *Debates* (Hansard), 25 October, 28295–99.

———. Special Committee on Election Expenses. 1971. "Minutes of Proceedings and Evidence." Third Session, 28th Parliament, 13:21.

Canadian Alliance for Trade and Job Opportunities. 1989. *The Canadian Alliance for Trade and Job Opportunities: Report of Activities March 1987 To March 1989*.

Common Cause. 1981. "A Common Cause Guide to Money, Power and Politics in the 97th Congress." Washington, DC.

———. 1984. "Looking to Purchase or Rent." Washington, DC.

———. 1986. "Financing the Finance Committee." Washington, DC.

Conway, M. Margaret. 1983. "PACs, the New Politics, and Congressional Campaigns." In *Interest Group Politics*, ed. Allan Gigler and Burdett Loomis. Washington, DC: Congressional Quarterly Press.

Côté, Pierre F. 1989. "Notes prepared for a panel discussion on the 11th annual conference of the Council on Governmental Ethics Laws." December, New Orleans.

Drew, Elizabeth. 1982. A Reporter at Large, "Politics and Money – I." *New Yorker*, 6 December, 54–149.

———. 1983. *Politics and Money: The New Road to Corruption*. New York: Macmillan.

Eismeier, Theodore J., and Phillip Pollick. 1984. "Political Action Committees: Varieties of Organization and Strategy." In *Money and Politics in the United States: Financing Elections in the 1980s,* ed. Michael Malbin. Washington, DC. American Enterprise Institute for Public Policy Research.

Ewing, Keith. 1987. *The Funding of Political Parties in Britain.* Cambridge: Cambridge University Press.

Federal Election Commission (FEC) v. Furgatch 807 F.2d 857 (9th Cir. 1987).

Federal Election Commission (FEC) v. Massachusetts Citizens for Life (MCFL) 479 U.S. 238 (1986).

Finlayson, Jock. (Canadian Alliance for Trade and Job Opportunities). 1990. Letter to the author dated 27 September 1990.

First National Bank of Boston v. Bellotti 435 U.S. 765 (1978).

Ford v. Quebec (Attorney General), [1988] 2 S.C.R. 712.

Globe and Mail. 1988. National Citizens' Coalition advertisement, 18 Nov.

―――. 1990. "Health Critics Seek Election Attention: Ontario Groups Urge More Financing, But Statistics Show Big Spending." 4 September, A6.

Grenzke, Janet. 1990. "Money and Congressional Behavior." In *Money, Elections, and Democracy: Reforming Congressional Campaign Finance,* ed. Margaret Latus Nugent and John Johannes. Boulder: Westview Press.

Gross, Kenneth. 1990. "Enhancing Enforcement." In *Money, Elections, and Democracy: Reforming Congressional Campaign Finance,* ed. Margaret Latus Nugent and John Johannes. Boulder: Westview Press.

Hailwood and Ackroyd Ltd. v. R., [1928] 2 K.B. 277.

Hiebert, Janet. 1989–90. "Fair Elections and Freedom of Expression under the Charter." *Journal of Canadian Studies* 24 (Winter): 72–86.

Irwin Toy Ltd. v. Quebec (Attorney General), [1989] 1 S.C.R. 927.

Jenson, Jane. 1990. "Maximising Equity and Innovation in Canada's Elections." Issue paper prepared for the Royal Commission on Electoral Reform and Party Financing. Ottawa.

―――. 1991. "Innovation and Equity: The Impact of Public Funding." In *Comparative Issues in Party and Election Finance,* ed. F. Leslie Seidle. Vol. 4 of the research studies of the Royal Commission on Electoral Reform and Party Financing. Ottawa and Toronto: RCERPF/Dundurn.

Johnston, Richard. 1990. "The Volume and Impact of 'Third-Party' Advertising in the 1988 Election." Memo to the Royal Commission on Electoral Reform and Party Financing. Ottawa.

Johnston, Richard, André Blais, Henry Brady and Jean Crête. 1991. "Putting the Pieces Together."

Magleby, David, and Candice Nelson. 1990. *The Money Chase: Congressional Campaign Finance Reform*. Washington, DC: The Brookings Institution.

Masclet, Jean-Claude. 1989. *Droit électoral*. Paris: Presses Universitaires de France.

Matasar, Anne. 1986. *Corporate PACs and Federal Campaign Financing Laws: Use or Abuse of Power?* New York: Quorum Books.

Mutch, Robert. 1988. *Campaigns, Congress, and Courts: The Making of Federal Campaign Finance Law*. New York: Praeger.

National Citizens' Coalition Inc./Coalition nationale des citoyens inc. v. Canada (Attorney General), [1984] 5 W.W.R. 436 (Alta. Q.B.).

New York Times Inc. v. Sullivan 376 U.S. 254 (1963).

Nova Scotia. *Elections Act*, R.S.N.S. 1989, c. 140, s. 3.

Parr, Judith. 1990. Letter to the Royal Commission on Electoral Reform and Party Financing from the Director of Communications, Alberta Federal and Intergovernmental Affairs. 18 December 1990.

Pinto-Duschinsky, Michael. 1989. "Trends in British Political Funding, 1979–84." In *Comparative Political Finance in the 1980s*, ed. Herbert Alexander. Cambridge: Cambridge University Press.

Quebec. *Charter of human rights and freedoms*, R.S.Q. c. C-12.

———. *Charter of the French language*, R.S.Q. c. C-11.

———. *Election Act*, R.S.Q. c. E-3.3, ss. 404, 413.

R. v. Edwards Books and Art Ltd., [1986] 2 S.C.R. 713.

R. v. Keegstra (1990), 1 C.R. (4th) 129 (S.C.C.).

R. v. Oakes, [1986] 1 S.C.R. 103.

R. v. Roach, Provincial Court (Criminal Division) Judicial District of York, Toronto, 24 Oct. 1977; affirmed (1978), 25 O.R. (2d) 767 (Co. Ct.).

R. v. Smith, [1987] 1 S.C.R. 1045.

R. v. Tronah Mines, [1952] 1 All E.R. 697.

Reiche, Frank. 1990. "Weakness of the FEC." In *Money, Elections, and Democracy: Reforming Congressional Campaign Finance*, ed. Margaret Latus Nugent and John Johannes. Boulder: Westview Press.

Roberge v. Québec (Procureur general), Superior Court, Montreal, 05-004628-804, 16 April 1980.

Sabato, Larry. 1987. "Real and Imagined Corruption in Campaign Financing." In *Elections American Style*, ed. A. James Reichley. Washington, DC: The Brookings Institution.

———. 1990. "PACs and Parties." In *Money, Elections and Democracy: Reforming Congressional Campaign Finance*, ed. Margaret Latus Nugent and John Johannes. Boulder: Westview Press.

Salutin, Rick. 1989. *Waiting for Democracy: A Citizen's Journal.* Toronto: Viking Press.

Saskatchewan. *The Election Act*, R.S.S. 1978, c. E-6, s. 231; en. 1978 (Supp.), c. 23, s. 26.

Seidle, F. Leslie, and Khayyam Zev Paltiel. 1981. "Party Finance, the Election Expenses Act, and Campaign Spending in 1979 and 1980." In *Canada at the Polls, 1979 and 1980*, ed. H.R. Penniman. Washington, DC: American Enterprise Institute for Public Policy Research.

Stewart, John B. 1977. *The Canadian House of Commons: Procedure and Reform.* Montreal: McGill-Queen's University Press.

Toronto Star. 1988. "Pro-Lifers Use Shock Literature, Photos in Last-Minute Blitz on Metro Ridings." 20 November, A4.

Traynor, Ken. (Pro-Canada Network). 1990. Letter to Royal Commission on Electoral Reform and Party Financing. 5 November.

Twentieth Century Fund. Task Force on Political Action Committees. 1984. *What Price PACs?* New York: Twentieth Century Fund.

United Kingdom. *Constitution Act, 1867*, 30 & 31 Vict., c. 3.

———. *Representation of the People Act 1983*, 1983, c. 2, s. 75.

United States. *Federal Election Campaign Act of 1971*, Pub. L. 92-225, Feb. 7, 1972.

———. *Code of Federal Regulations*, 109.2. Federal Elections, Washington: Officer of the Federal Register, National Archives and Records Administration, Jan. 1, 1990, 100–101.

United States. Federal Election Commission. 1989. Press Release. 9 April.

United States v. Pipefitters 407 U.S. 385 (1972).

Walls, Lorne. (Canadian Alliance for Trade and Job Opportunities). 1990. Letter to Royal Commission on Electoral Reform and Party Financing. 5 November 1990.

Weinrib, Lorraine. 1988. "The Supreme Court of Canada and Section One of the Charter." *Supreme Court Law Review* 10:469–513.

Wright, John R. 1990. "Contributions, Lobbying, and Committee Voting in the U.S. House of Representatives." *American Political Science Review* 84:417–38.

2

POLITICAL ACTIVITY OF LOCAL INTEREST GROUPS

A. Brian Tanguay
Barry J. Kay

IN RECENT YEARS a swelling chorus of criticism – from academics, journalists and politicians alike – has been directed at the election activities of organized interest groups. There is a widespread perception that these rapidly proliferating groups – representing such diverse interests as business, labour, agriculture, women, natives, ethnic and linguistic minorities, abortion activists (pro-choice and pro-life), welfare recipients, the physically and mentally disabled, consumers, advocates of nuclear disarmament, environmentalists and others – are becoming better organized and more overtly political. Some groups have considerable resources at their disposal and are more than willing to spend freely at election time to promote their interests or to support political parties and candidates favourable to their cause. Other groups rely on aggressive public relations campaigns or media stunts to get their message across to politicians and voters. Whatever the tactics employed, there is a growing fear that these groups may influence electoral outcomes by hijacking the political agenda and thereby diminishing the role of the traditional representative institutions in a democracy – political parties.

One influential lobbying firm recently captured the public mood of fear and hostility to organized interests with the following lament:

> Throughout the 1980s, single interest groups and groups representing coalitions of interests have been growing in strength and number. These are becoming better organized and highly politicized.
>
> Ontario's David Peterson was one victim of this phenomenon. He

was badgered and hounded by community groups and interest groups throughout his election campaign. As he put it after his defeat, his deathblow was not a single killing thrust; he died "the death of a thousand cuts", each administered by a different interest group. (Public Affairs International 1990, 37–38)

Complaints about the pernicious influence of organized interest groups reached a crescendo in the aftermath of the 1988 federal election, when various coalitions opposing the Free Trade Agreement accused big business of "buying" the Tories' election win.[1] Academic critics of existing election expenses legislation at the federal level contended that the "unaccountable and unregulated campaign spending by wealthy interest groups" during the 1988 election had undermined the democratic process by giving too great a voice to well-heeled business groups (Hiebert 1989–90, 82). These critics worry that in the absence of strict regulation of "third-party" spending during elections, the door is open to the malignant Political Action Committee (PAC) virus from the United States.[2] This, they fear, could lead to government by special interests, as political parties and individual candidates become increasingly beholden to a few wealthy groups with a great deal of money to propagate their views (Paltiel 1987, 236).

Much of the literature on the election activities of organized interests focuses on politics at the federal or provincial level. At these levels, high-profile groups tend to be quite politicized and adept at manipulating the media to pressure elected officials or to mobilize public support. Surprisingly little has been written about interest group activities at the local level (the constituency). It is this lacuna that our study seeks to fill. Our research is largely exploratory, consisting of a series of interviews with interest group representatives in a sample of federal constituencies. The questionnaire administered to these groups included items on the organizational structure, resources and objectives of the groups, the nature and extent of their electoral participation, their public relations activities in non-election periods and their own assessment of the responsiveness of the political system to their concerns. We also asked the interest groups to outline any reforms that they felt might be necessary to make the political system more responsive to local groups like theirs. (This section of the questionnaire included an item specifically asking the group's view on whether organized interests ought to be allowed to provide money or other resources to candidates or parties favourable to their objectives.) Finally, the members of Parliament in the ridings selected for study – or their constituency officers, if the MP was unavailable – were interviewed. MPs were asked about the nature and extent of their contacts with interest groups, the amount of time they devoted to dealing with these groups and their assessment of the effectiveness of the political activities of organized interests (both during and between elections).

The overarching policy questions to be considered in our study include whether local interest groups believe that they receive a fair hearing from the candidates and the media in the existing electoral process, whether they see themselves as having a meaningful impact on this process, what the correlates of perceived policy influence are and whether reforms need to be implemented to make the system more equitable.

One of our principal concerns is to determine whether the popular portrait of excessively politicized, militantly self-serving and influential interest groups increasingly found in the media is an accurate depiction at the local level. We note at the outset that independent research recently conducted on the abortion issue casts doubt on the ability of organized groups on either side of the issue to mobilize significant numbers of voters (Kay et al. 1989). It may be, then, that the perils of "government by special interest" have been overstated by pundits and politicians, that the ability of interest groups to influence electoral outcomes is less than popularly believed and that factors specific to the Canadian system make it unlikely that the American PAC phenomenon will become as virulent in this country.

The remainder of this study is organized into seven sections. The first section outlines some of the difficulties encountered in drawing our sample of interest groups and provides an overview of the questionnaire design employed in the survey. Section two examines criteria for classifying interest groups – in particular, Paul Pross's (1986) notion of institutionalization – and sketches the typology we adopted. The third section examines the strategies employed by our sample of interest groups to contact and influence local, provincial and federal politicians, as well as the public. In this section we also discuss the interest groups' perceptions of their political effectiveness and of the responsiveness of the political system to their concerns. Section four is a case study of Campaign Life, one of the most widely discussed interest group campaigns during the 1988 federal election. The fifth section focuses on interest groups' proposals for making the political system more responsive to their demands at the local level. In this section we note their thoughts on third-party spending during election campaigns. Section six consists of a brief discussion of the attitudes of local members of Parliament toward interest groups and their activities at the constituency level. The concluding section discusses the implications of our findings for electoral reform.

SAMPLE AND METHODOLOGY

Because of the lack of systematic research into the election activities of local interest groups in Canada, the primary objective of this study was to survey as broad a cross-section of these organizations as practicable. Initially, we had hoped to adhere to the principles of random selection as closely as possible and draw a sample of federal constituencies from Quebec, Ontario, Saskatchewan and Alberta. Time constraints made it impossible to extend the survey to the entire nation, although an abortive attempt was made to add a Nova Scotian riding to the sample.[3] An effort was also made to include large urban, smaller urban and rural electoral districts, as well as to ensure a partisan balance among the ridings (roughly equivalent to the strength of each party in the House of Commons). These efforts, however, had to be modified considerably because many MPs were reluctant to cooperate and in some cases were openly hostile. This lack of cooperation ultimately forced us to select some constituencies not on the basis of their demographic characteristics or the party affiliation of the sitting MP, but simply because the local MP was willing to assist us.

Table 2.1
Distribution of interest group interviews, by riding

Riding	Sitting MP	Urban* (%)	Groups interviewed	
			N	%
Edmonton Northwest	PC	100.0	8	9.0
Edmonton East	NDP	100.0	10	11.2
Saskatoon–Clark's Crossing	NDP	85.8	9	10.1
Kindersley–Lloydminster	PC	7.7	1	1.1
Kent	Lib	61.3	6	6.7
Waterloo	PC	92.1	11	12.4
Hastings–Frontenac– Lennox and Addington	PC	0.0	5	5.6
Kingston and the Islands	Lib	90.2	13	14.6
Leeds–Grenville	Lib	38.9	7	7.9
Lachine–Lac-Saint-Louis	PC	100.0	7	7.9
Blainville–Deux Montagnes	PC	100.0	5	5.6
Saint-Henri–Westmount	Lib	100.0	7	7.9
Total			89	100.0

*Percentage of polling districts within each constituency that were classified as urban. See Canada, *Elections Canada* (1988).

Twelve federal ridings were eventually selected: three in Quebec, five in Ontario, two in Saskatchewan and two in Alberta. Seven of these ridings are urban (with more than 90 percent of the polling districts classified as urban by the *Report of the Chief Electoral Officer*), two are urban with significant rural components (more than 10 percent of the polls) and three are predominantly rural (see table 2.1). As for the party affiliation of the incumbent MPs in the twelve constituencies, six are Progressive Conservatives, four are Liberals and two are members of the NDP.

Within each constituency we sought to draw a representative sample of interest groups that had been in contact with their MP at any time during or after the 1988 federal election. In each riding we approached the MP – or the MP's constituency officers – and asked for a list of such organizations and contact people we could interview. In most cases the MP was happy to comply. In a few instances, however, the MP balked. Some expressed the fear that our data might be used for malicious or mischievous purposes – to attempt to smear them with charges of patronage, for example. Despite our repeated assurances that the information would be treated with the utmost confidentiality, and that this was not a muckraking exercise, we were unable to obtain their cooperation. Other MPs professed not to know what interest groups were, or claimed that they rarely or *never* had any contacts with such organizations (one Metro Toronto Progressive Conservative MP actually made this claim!). Still others begged off because of their busy schedules.

Despite this lack of cooperation from some members of Parliament, we were able to obtain lists of interest groups for the 12 ridings in our sample. From the lists provided by the MPs, we selected 89 organizations for interviews (the complete list of interest groups is found in appendix A). To ensure as broad a cross-section of these groups as possible – from well-established and wealthy groups to relatively new ones – we had to undertake a certain amount of purposive selection. We make no claim, therefore, that the sample is random, nor that the findings can be generalized to all interest groups. But since little work has been done in this area, this type of exploratory research is crucial.

It should be noted that some of the MPs' lists were more complete, up-to-date and reliable than others. This is likely accounted for by the fact that not every interest group that was selected for an interview had had contact with its local MP since the 1988 federal election. In fact, of the 89 groups interviewed, 9 (10.1 percent) had not contacted their federal MP since the last election.

As table 2.1 indicates, the number of interest groups interviewed

Table 2.2
Distribution of interest group interviews, by region

	Interest groups interviewed	
Region	N	%
West	28	31.5
Ontario	42	47.2
Quebec	19	21.3
Total	89	100.0

in each riding varied considerably, from 1 in Kindersley–Lloydminster (Saskatchewan) to 13 in Kingston and the Islands (Ontario). The extremely low number in Kindersley–Lloydminster is explained by the logistical difficulties that confronted the interviewer. Tracking down small organizations – which frequently had no telephone, merely a post office box number – in distant parts of this sprawling rural riding was too time-consuming and expensive, and the task had to be abandoned. Because of the extreme variations in the number of interest group interviews in each riding, statistical calculations in the following analysis are based on the region in which the group is located. In this manner, the distribution is much less distorted (see table 2.2).

The questionnaire contained some 50 questions, both closed- and open-ended, on each group's organizational structure, the nature and frequency of its contacts with various levels of government, its public relations strategies and the extent of its satisfaction with the political system. (A copy of the questionnaire can be found in appendix B.) In most cases (74 of 89), the interviews were conducted in person; in the remaining instances (usually in rural ridings where many groups were scattered over a wide area), they were conducted by telephone.

It was our initial intention to interview elected MPs, their staff (including the campaign manager), other candidates and representatives of the local media, in addition to the interest groups themselves. Largely as a result of the difficulties we encountered in trying to track many of these people down, we were forced to abandon this intention. Instead, we attempted to conduct personal interviews with the twelve MPs in the ridings chosen for our sample (the questionnaire can be found in appendix C). Five consented to an interview, and two had their political aides responsible for constituency affairs fill out the questionnaires and mail them to us. The remaining five MPs were either unavailable (some were out of the country for extended periods) or ignored our request. This extremely small sample of interviews greatly restricts our ability to make generalizations about MPs' attitudes toward local interest group involvement in the electoral and political process. Nonetheless, information gleaned from these interviews should prove helpful in pointing the way toward future research.

CLASSIFICATION OF LOCAL INTEREST GROUPS

There is no single, widely accepted scheme for classifying interest groups. Probably the best known typology in the Canadian literature on this subject is that of Paul Pross (1986, chap. 5) who employs the concepts of organizational capacity and institutionalization to classify interest groups. According to Pross, most interest groups pass through an organizational life cycle, beginning their existence as relatively ill-equipped, underfinanced and naïve coalitions concerned with "the resolution of one or two issues or problems" (ibid., 117). They tend to seek publicity or media attention more than access to key political decision makers. Their relations with government, to the extent that they exist, are sporadic and unsophisticated. The achievement of their short-term objectives tends to take precedence over the exigencies of organizational growth. If these groups successfully adapt to the political system, they expand their membership base, increase their knowledge of the workings of government, enter into frequent and intimate contact with those agencies of the state relevant to their concerns and place organizational growth and survival ahead of any single objective (ibid., 114–16). This framework yields a four-fold typology, with "issue-oriented" groups at one end of the organizational continuum and fully "institutionalized" groups at the other. "Fledgling" and "mature" groups lie between these two poles.

Pross's emphasis on the organizational attributes of interest groups and the mode of their interaction with the state is a useful contribution to the study of pressure politics. As a result, our questionnaire includes many items designed to measure the degree of institutionalization of a given group: age, size of membership, annual budget, size of paid staff and objectives (single-issue or multiple). However, for the purpose of our study, there are aspects of Pross's typology that are less helpful. In particular, its treatment of single-issue groups leaves a great deal to be desired, since it assumes that as groups achieve a high degree of organizational sophistication they abandon "the frenetic, publicity-seeking behaviour" characteristic of non-institutionalized groups (Pross 1986, 126). Yet, as the activities of Greenpeace, Sea Shepherd and similar organizations attest, this is not always the case. Pross labels these groups

Table 2.3
Classification of local interest groups

	N	%
Business	13	14.6
Labour-agricultural	6	6.7
Moral-ethical	9	10.1
Social service	45	50.6
Noneconomic interests	10	11.2
Environmental and consumer	6	6.7
Total	89	99.9*

*Does not total 100% because of rounding.

"analytical conundrums," and he is compelled to resort to ad hoc explanations to account for their confrontational and anything-but-discreet relations with government. This is a serious shortcoming in Pross's typology: it is unable to explain adequately the behaviour of groups that operate outside the conventions of traditional pressure politics. It is precisely these groups, moreover, that Public Affairs International, in the quotation cited at the beginning of this study, was singling out as "badgering and hounding" former Ontario Liberal Premier David Peterson, driving him from office.

Groups like Greenpeace, Sea Shepherd and the pro-life committees refuse to play the game of pressure politics in the manner stipulated by Pross because their objectives are qualitatively different from those of other organizations. They are reflections of an emerging "new political paradigm" (Offe 1987, 66–76) that stresses issues such as autonomy, identity, and the preservation of the environment and of humanity. This is in stark contrast to the old paradigm's preoccupation with economic growth, distribution and security. Each political paradigm privileges different modes of interaction with the state: traditional pressure politics and lobbying in the old paradigm, confrontation and extraparliamentary action in the new.

To capture this dimension of interest group life, we have categorized groups primarily by their stated objectives: those that represent and defend the interests of their own membership, those that provide a service to the broader community, and those that seek to change the prevailing pattern or definition of politics and to convince the public of the need for such a change. Our initial hypothesis is that each of

Table 2.4
Group type with size of budget

	Type (%)					
Budget dollars	Business	Labour	Moral	Social services	Non-economic	Environmental
< 100 000	—	100.0	77.8	24.4	50.0	60.0
100 000 – 999 999	69.2	—	22.2	46.7	20.0	—
> 1 million	30.8	—	—	28.9	30.0	40.0

Note: This table, and all the others that follow, employ column percentages.
Lambda = .31, $p < .000$.

these types of groups will interact differently with the state *because* of its specific objective. Into the first broad category of associational interest fall business, labour and agricultural groups. Also included are groups representing ethnic, linguistic and native communities (labelled "non-economic interests" in our typology). As table 2.3 indicates, these groups constitute respectively 14.6%, 6.7% and 11.2% of our sample.[4] Social service groups constitute a category by themselves, equivalent to more than half of the entire sample (50.6%). In the final category are those attempting to change the definition of politics. There we have placed two distinct types of groups: those with moral-ethical concerns, which seek to promote a particular viewpoint on a moral or ethical question (such as the pro-life and pro-choice committees, and Project Ploughshares), and those representing environmental or consumer interests.[5] Respectively, these two categories account for 10.1% and 6.7% of our sample (see table 2.3).

Tables 2.4, 2.5, 2.6 and 2.7 provide data on the organizational attributes of these different interest groups. It is worth noting that there are, roughly speaking, two organizational clusters. At one end of the spectrum are the labour and moral-ethical groups, operating with limited budgets, little or no government funding, a small paid staff but a large membership. Data on this last characteristic are not shown in the tables. These groups frequently forge ties with other similar groups in their riding. At the opposite end are the business and social service groups, operating with big budgets, substantial government funding (more than 60 percent of business groups get more than half of their revenue from government sources; in the case of social service groups, this figure is just under 80 percent) and large paid staffs. The non-economic interest groups tend to resemble these wealthier groups but have fewer resources. Environmental groups

Table 2.5
Group type with government revenue

Revenue from government (%)	Type (%)					
	Business	Labour	Moral	Social services	Non-economic	Environmental
0	23.1	100.0	77.8	8.9	40.0	33.3
1–50	15.4	—	11.1	13.3	40.0	16.7
> 50	61.5	—	11.1	77.8	20.0	50.0

Lambda = .35, $p < .000$.

Table 2.6
Group type with size of paid staff

Size of paid staff	Type (%)					
	Business	Labour	Moral	Social services	Non-economic	Environmental
0	—	50.0	55.6	2.2	50.0	33.3
1–5	61.5	50.0	33.3	24.4	20.0	33.3
6–10	15.4	—	11.1	22.2	—	16.7
11+	23.1	—	—	51.1	30.0	16.7

Lambda = .27, $p < .000$.

tend to be a breed apart: 60 percent of them have relatively small budgets; they are small and have limited paid staff, few volunteers and limited ties to similar groups in their community. Half of these groups, however, do receive more than 50 percent of their revenue from government sources.

LOCAL INTEREST GROUPS: STRATEGIES FOR POLITICAL INTERVENTION

This section of the study examines strategies employed by interest groups for contacting and influencing local, provincial and federal politicians, as well as the general public. The first subsection considers the groups' different assessments of the effectiveness of their activities, and of the responsiveness of the political system to their concerns. This is followed by a more detailed examination of the different patterns of group activity – the frequency and nature of contacts with politicians and the media.

Table 2.7
Group type working with other similar groups

Does your group work with other similar groups?	Type (%)					
	Business	Labour	Moral	Social services	Non-economic	Environmental
No	63.6	25.0	14.3	54.1	44.4	66.7
Yes	36.4	75.0	85.7	45.9	55.6	33.3

Lambda = .20, p = .30.

Group Perceptions of Politics

The level of satisfaction with which local interest groups view the political system has been measured in many ways. Because our study was organized through contacts provided by members of Parliament, questions about those MPs provide a baseline for evaluating elements of the political system.

More than three-quarters of interest groups who responded were very or somewhat satisfied with their federal MP's response (50 percent were very satisfied). This proportion compares favourably with the approval rates for provincial and local elected officials, where 33 and 27 percent respectively of groups were very satisfied with their representatives. This point should not be overemphasized, since the sample design was likely to identify groups in contact with their MP, and the number of groups totally dissatisfied with their representatives did not vary greatly across the different levels of government. However, the evidence does tend to refute the suggestion that federal MPs are less responsive to local interest groups, even though they sit in a more distant location and usually have greater time constraints. It might be added that federal MPs are approached in different ways (letter, personal meeting, telephone, demonstration) more frequently than provincial or local representatives are. The only exceptions were provincial legislators, who were contacted slightly more frequently by phone, and municipal representatives, who had personal meetings somewhat more often.

The substantial level of satisfaction with federal members of Parliament does not, however, extend to the political system at large. In contrast to the 50% of the sample who were very satisfied with their MP, only 8% were very satisfied with the way the political system in general responded to their group's concerns. This relative support for individual representatives, combined with criticism of the system as a whole, is consistent with several studies of the U.S. Congress (Fenno 1990). Satisfaction with the current federal government was even lower (less than 5% were very satisfied, and 72% claimed to be dissatisfied). Contentment with political parties on the whole, both federal and provincial, was low. Only the NDP achieved a proportion of more than 10% of the groups that were very satisfied or less than 50% that were dissatisfied. Local government received a "very satisfied" rating from only 15% of the sample, although the "somewhat satisfied" evaluation was modal for this level of government.

Questions that asked respondents for relative assessments of how their group is treated in comparison with others also showed a more positive ranking for the MP compared to the federal political system. In addition, provincial and local government levels were perceived as somewhat more favourable to interest groups than was the federal government. However, on every item dealing with relative treatment, there were more group representatives who saw themselves doing worse than the norm rather than better. In the case of the federal government, 63 percent of groups thought that they were treated worse than the norm, and 9 percent thought that they were treated better. It may not be surprising that a majority of the sample thought that other interest groups had too much influence in the political process. This sentiment was unanimous among moral-ethical groups but less evident for those concerned with social service issues.

To be more specific, business-oriented interest groups were most likely to be satisfied with their MP, government, political system in general and public response to their message. On the other hand, the environmental-consumer groups were the least satisfied, particularly with regard to their MP and the political system. Among the other group classifications, differences in the level of satisfaction were less significant. With regard to government level, social service groups tended to rank the provincial government as more supportive than the federal government, and business groups rated local government highest. Otherwise, the differences by level were not significant.

Group resources had a clear relationship with the level of satisfaction. Satisfaction correlated more consistently with interest groups' budget size than with any other group trait (Kendall tau of .3 and gamma of .5). This observation ran through the gamut of satisfaction questions, including perceptions of the MP, the political system, different levels of government, the media, political parties and rankings of relative treatment.

There was a substantial degree of multicollinearity apparent between a group's budget and characteristics such as the group's age, membership size, number of paid staff and proportion of revenue that comes from government. Each of these variables tended to be positively associated with most measures of political satisfaction. This suggests that the groups most dissatisfied tended to be less established, smaller in membership and paid staff, and did not receive much revenue from government. Although there was a general association between the number of paid staff employed by a group and its level of political satisfaction, there was little relationship between the size of volunteer staff and the different measures of satisfaction.

More detailed observations are pertinent for the purpose of amplification. The newer interest groups (those in existence less than five years) were more than twice as likely to be dissatisfied with their member of Parliament than long-term groups (those established for 20 years or more). Despite this, however, the fledgling groups were less likely to bypass their MP by appealing directly to the Cabinet or bureaucracy. This seems to indicate that less established groups either lack the sophistication and experience needed to deal effectively with the political system, or they lack faith in traditional patterns of pressure politics.

Most interest groups did not distinguish in partisan terms in their evaluations of government and parties. They were either critical or supportive across the board, with one exception. Labour groups strongly favoured the NDP, although they were quite dissatisfied with alternative political elements, including nonpartisan factors such as the media.

Finally, it should be noted that political satisfaction is inversely related to the question of third-party election spending. This point should not be overstated because the numbers were not always significant. But groups that are presently dissatisfied, in part because of their low level of resources, are most in favour of relatively free election spending. Ironically, it is frequently argued that these less advantaged groups probably have less influence on the system than do the better funded groups that are opposed to change.

Tables 2.8 and 2.9 provide data on how groups perceive their member of Parliament and the political system in general.

Table 2.8
Group type with perception of MP

Perception of MP	Type (%)					
	Business	Labour	Moral	Social services	Non-economic	Environmental
Very satisfied	76.9	40.0	55.6	51.2	40.0	0.0
Somewhat satisfied	23.1	40.0	11.1	24.4	20.0	66.7
Not satisfied	0.0	20.0	33.3	24.4	40.0	33.3

Lambda = .05.

Table 2.9
Group type with perception of a political system

Political system	Business	Labour	Moral	Social services	Non-economic	Environmental
				Type (%)		
Very satisfied	38.5	0.0	0.0	5.0	0.0	0.0
Somewhat satisfied	38.5	20.0	22.2	62.5	40.0	16.7
Not satisfied	23.1	80.0	77.8	32.5	60.0	83.3

Lambda = .19.

Group Patterns of Political Activity

Contacts between interest groups and federal MPs varied substantially in frequency, with some groups mentioning more than 100 contacts since the 1988 election. At the other end of the continuum, 10 percent of the sample claimed that they had not contacted their member of Parliament in the two years since the previous federal election, despite the fact that they were recommended for interviews by the MPs (a possible explanation of this is found in the section on methodology). The remaining groups fell into approximately equal proportions of those who had contacted their MP once a year, two or three times a year and more than three times a year.

The most common method of contacting was by mail, an approach used by 75 percent of the sample, followed by personal meetings at just over 60 percent. Relatively few groups used the telephone or demonstrations as methods of contacting. Given the level of satisfaction with their MPs, it is interesting to note that a substantial number of groups had mentioned going over the heads of their elected representatives, at least on occasion. There was a large non-response on this item; however, fully two-thirds of those responding to the question and at least 40 percent of the total sample mentioned going directly to the Cabinet or federal bureaucracy at times (most specified the Cabinet). This tends to reflect a widespread awareness of the actual operation of the political system, in which an MP does not always have great influence.

As noted previously, contact with provincial and local representatives was less frequent than with MPs. The 1988 general election did provide an opportunity for contacting the various candidates. Candidates from the three main parties were approached by portions of the sample ranging from 21% to 30%, but less than 5% of the sample actually supported any specific party's candidate, a total of 12% of the sample that was active in a partisan way. Having noted this, less than 20% of the groups indicated that during the election campaign they used means other than contacting their MP to pursue their objectives.

Every group interviewed saw public education as a means of attaining its objectives. However, individual contacting (74%) and the print media (67%) were clearly the most commonly used methods to contact the public, with television and radio much less frequently mentioned. Comments from some interest group leaders would suggest that it is left to the national headquarters or parent organization (where one exists) to use these more expensive electronic media. General satisfaction with media coverage was apparent, with 32% of the sample very satisfied and an additional 48% somewhat satisfied, although 20% were dissatisfied. Similarly, there was satisfaction with the public's response to the group's message: 38% very satisfied, 45% somewhat satisfied and 17% dissatisfied.

Distinctive behaviour among the various interest groups appeared to be linked to their political perceptions. Environmental groups, which were the most dissatisfied with the political system and the actors within it, were also less involved in contacting politicians than the others, even in contacting the NDP. One-half of these environmental groups had no direct contact with MPs at all. This suggests a relative absence of efficacy, a lack of political sophistication or a lack of faith in traditional forms of politics. By contrast, groups dealing with moral or ethical issues, although not particularly well funded, have been very active in making political contacts and have also been much more satisfied with the process.

Other findings indicate that business and noneconomic interest groups were busiest at making political contacts in most of the activities measured. The business group also most frequently reported contacts initiated by the MP. One exception to this trend was in contacts with the NDP, in which labour and agricultural groups were most active. Social service groups tended to be less active in regular contacts but, unlike the environmental groups, were much more content with the system. Groups included in the moral-ethical category, such as those concerned with abortion, were most likely to change their tactics during elections. No business group mentioned a change in tactics during elections and they were uniformly nonconfrontational in their approach.

It is interesting to note that the size of a group's budget, although positively associated with political satisfaction, had an inverse relationship with many contacting activities. This was particularly true of less orthodox confrontational approaches. This finding corresponds to the expectations about the behaviour of established groups generated by Pross's typology. Members of Parliament were also much more likely to initiate contacts with high-budget groups, another finding consistent with Pross's framework. Organizations that received greater government revenue were less likely to initiate contact, a factor particularly evident among the large number of social service groups receiving government support.

The better-established groups and those with larger memberships tended to be somewhat more active in contacting, particularly in media activity, but this pattern was inconsistent. Larger groups were more likely to have a distinctive election strategy and to be approached by MPs. The size of a group's paid staff seemed to have little relationship with contacting, but the number of volunteer workers did tend to have a link with several activities. There was little evidence that groups behaved differently because they shared goals with other organizations.

Among the specific political activities in which correlations existed was the frequency of MP contact with a special election strategy, frequency of media contacts in general and specific use of the print media. The act of going over the head of an MP by appealing directly to Cabinet or federal bureaucracy was also linked to many of these same activities, including distinctive electoral behaviour and use of the print media.

To the extent that a pattern can be discerned, it appears that the various acts of political contacting by local interest groups, whether involving media or direct approaches to party representatives, are not isolated behaviours but part of a cluster of similar activities. Moreover, it appears that activities involving greater sophistication, such as distinctive election behaviour or bypassing the MP, are likewise undertaken by groups as part of a generalized political orientation. In summary, there was a tendency for groups most active in contacting to favour a system that would enhance their independent campaign activity during elections. However, the evidence on this matter is not always consistent or significant.

Tables 2.10 and 2.11 provide data on the frequency of contacting by different types of groups, as well as their incidences of employing a different strategy during elections.

CASE STUDY: CAMPAIGN LIFE IN THE 1988 ELECTION

Having reviewed how local interest groups interact with the political system, we now provide a case study of the most widespread interest group campaign during the 1988 federal election at the constituency level. It was the activity of Campaign Life to promote a right-to-life anti-abortion position and to endorse candidates across party lines who supported its position.

Table 2.10
Group type with frequency of contacting MP

Contacting MP	Type (%)					
	Business	Labour	Moral	Social services	Non-economic	Environmental
> 3	46.2	50.0	33.3	22.2	60.0	16.7
2–3	15.4	16.7	66.7	28.9	30.0	16.7
1	30.8	33.3	0.0	37.8	10.0	16.7
Never	7.7	0.0	0.0	11.1	0.0	50.0

Lambda = .12.

Table 2.11
Group type with different election strategy

Special election strategy	Type (%)					
	Business	Labour	Moral	Social services	Non-economic	Environmental
Yes	0	33.3	50.0	11.1	40.0	16.7
No	100	66.7	50.0	88.9	60.0	83.3

Lambda = .00.

In this pursuit, the most important resource was the November 1988 election edition of *Vitality*, a publication of the Coalition for the Protection of Human Life. It listed the positions on abortion of federal candidates from every riding in the country except New Brunswick, Yukon and the Northwest Territories. The publication's approval was bestowed primarily on those candidates who answered "yes" in writing to the question: "If elected, will you support measures to introduce and pass a law to protect every unborn child from the time of conception?" In addition, information was provided for incumbent MPs on parliamentary votes related to abortion, including the pro-life amendment proposed by Gus Mitges and defeated in a parliamentary free vote on 28 July 1988. This proposal would have restricted all abortions except when a mother's life was threatened. From this information, *Vitality* clearly indicated that the candidates it classified as pro-life supported Campaign Life's position on the abortion issue.

A comparison with the 1984 federal election is instructive, since the right-to-life movement did not launch a comparable campaign at that time and the abortion issue appeared to have a lower electoral pro-file before the Supreme Court decision. The research design made no assumptions about how widely Campaign Life's candidate evaluations were known. Part of the challenge faced by any such interest group was not only to make endorsements, but also to inform the public of those endorsements. Accordingly, if such a group failed to have an impact, it would not be clear whether that was a result of indifference or insufficient information among the electorate.

In total, 125 major party candidates were identified by the above procedure, including 74 Conservatives, 50 Liberals and 1 New Democrat. For each of these cases, the percentage change in the party vote for that particular constituency between 1984 and 1988 was calculated, and the province-wide swing for the party involved was then subtracted from this difference. This was done to determine the change in the vote for pro-life candidates compared with the previous election, after control-ling for the party's performance in that province. To illustrate, Tom Wappel, the pro-life Liberal candidate who ran in Scarborough West, won with 36.8% of the vote, a 7.2% improvement for his party com-pared with the same area in 1984. However, the entire Liberal perfor-mance in Ontario represented a 9.4% improvement compared with 1984. When this provincial swing was subtracted from the Scarborough West result, Wappel was shown to have performed 2.2% worse than the average Liberal in the province. Conversely Steven Woodworth, the pro-life Liberal in Waterloo, lost the election but ran 2.8% ahead of his party swing in Ontario.

In another example, widely trumpeted following the federal elec-tion, pro-choice Justice Minister Ray Hnatyshyn lost in Saskatoon–Clark's Crossing after Campaign Life supported his Liberal opponent Bill Patrick. Patrick performed 3.6 percent better than the average Liberal in Saskatchewan, but the pro-choice NDP candidate and eventual win-ner, Chris Axworthy, performed even better compared with his provin-cial party average. If one were to assume (probably erroneously) that the 3.6 percent was totally composed of pro-life voters, it could have been added to Hnatyshyn's total and the Justice Minister would still have lost by a substantial margin.

These examples represent only 3 of the 125 cases, and any given constituency outcome may be subject to many idiosyncratic circum-stances that make it atypical of more general trends. However, it seems reasonable to assume that if the Campaign Life endorsement had sig-nificant political impact, it should become evident when comparing the entire performance of the 125 pro-life candidates with colleagues in their respective parties who did not gain the group's support. Among the full complement of pro-life candidates, 67 did better than their fellow party candidates within their province, 56 did worse and another 2 performed at the level of their party's provincial support. When the adjusted percentage swing for all 125 pro-life candidates was averaged, the mean was .35 of one percentage point, not a level significant beyond statistical chance. The distinctions between endorsed Conservative and Liberal party members were slight. One must conclude from this that Campaign Life's endorsement during the 1988 federal election campaign did not provide a significant benefit to those 125 major-party candidates that were identified.

One other illustration of an interest group targeting candidates is that of the National Citizens' Coalition (NCC). During the 1988 federal election campaign, its opposition to the NDP involved spending $150 000 to broadcast advertisements mostly in Manitoba, Saskatchewan and British Columbia. (The NCC spent another $700 000 during the pre-election period [see Hiebert 1991].) In the 41 western ridings targeted by the NCC, however, the NDP actually performed an average of 1.8 percent better than in the 19 remaining ridings not targeted in those provinces. It might be noted that following the election, despite these results, the NCC issued a press release claiming victory in its campaign.

INTEREST GROUP PROPOSALS FOR POLITICAL REFORM

As noted in the subsection on group perceptions of politics, a substantial proportion of interest groups in our survey were dissatisfied with the political system and the way in which it responded to their demands, although local members of Parliament, for the most part, were exempt from this criticism. An indication of interest group dissatisfaction with the responsiveness of the political system was also found in answers to the question: "Do you think that there are any other local groups that have too much influence in the political process?" Sixty percent of the organizations responding to this question (51 out of 85) agreed that there were other groups that wielded too much influence, although 40 percent (34 out of 85) disagreed. When asked to specify which groups they thought were too powerful, more than half (27 of 50) mentioned "business" or "wealthy" groups. The other groups mentioned more than once were single-issue groups (6 of 50), the bureaucracy (3 of 50) and women's groups (2 of 50).

To gauge the interest group's desire for political reform, one item in the questionnaire asked specifically whether local interest groups ought to be allowed to spend money on, or provide other resources for, candidates or parties favouring their cause. Another asked what reforms the groups would like to see implemented to make the political system more responsive to their concerns. On the third-party spending question, 50 of 85 groups (58.8 percent) stated that interest groups should *not* be allowed to spend money during elections to promote or oppose candidates and parties, although 35 groups (41.2 percent) felt that there should be no such restrictions. When asked to elaborate on the reasons for their answers, those opposed to third-party spending tended to say that it would lead to domination of the electoral and political processes by groups with the most money to spend. One business group representative said that he was opposed to third-party spending because there were "too many do-gooders in this country" eager to lavish money on their favourite hobby-horses and that the country could not afford this. One of the moral-ethical groups asserted that individuals within organizations should be free to support or oppose whomever they wished, however they wished, but that the organizations themselves should not be allowed to spend money during an election. A number of social service groups opposed to third-party spending observed that in many cases it is the government's, not the organization's, money that is spent to promote or oppose parties or candidates and that this practice is clearly unethical. They further claimed that since publicly funded groups (or those with charitable status) had their hands tied during an election, other groups should be subjected to similar constraints, rendering the playing field level. Still other groups were fearful that third-party spending would leave organizations vulnerable to reprisal from an elected representative if it became known that they had supported a losing candidate. Among their fears were that they might be frozen out of important community projects or ignored during the consultative process.

Of the groups in favour of third-party spending, the most common reason given was that any attempt to prohibit this would be an infringement of freedom of speech. One representative from a moral-ethical group argued that such spending can be of significant help to non-élite, non-establishment groups trying to break into the political process. Of the 35 groups that did not oppose third-party spending, however, it is interesting to note that a substantial number (10) added the qualification that either there should be some mechanism for guaranteeing disclosure of monetary sources (since parties and candidates are subject to these constraints) or limits should be placed on spending to ensure that the more affluent groups do not dominate the electoral process.

There were some interesting variations in support for or opposition to third-party spending, as tables 2.12 through 2.18 indicate. Groups in Quebec were overwhelmingly opposed to third-party spending during elections, with almost 90 percent supporting a ban on this activity. A solid majority of groups in the two western provinces (63 percent) were

Table 2.12
Attitudes toward third-party spending, by region

Should groups be allowed to spend?	Region (%)		
	West	Ontario	Quebec
No	63.0	41.0	89.5
Yes	37.0	59.0	10.5

Lambda = .20, $p < .05$.

Table 2.13
Attitudes toward third-party spending, by type of group

Should groups be allowed to spend?	Type (%)					
	Business	Labour	Moral	Social services	Non-economic	Environmental
No	53.8	16.7	44.4	69.8	66.7	40.0
Yes	46.2	83.3	55.6	30.2	33.3	60.0

Lambda = .17, $p = .14$.

also opposed, but Ontario was the lone region in which a majority of groups (59 percent) had no objection to this practice. We do not wish to make too much of this finding, since it could have been influenced by a host of variables. Nevertheless, it could be suggested that Quebec's distinctive election financing law of 1977, allowing only individual electors to contribute to political parties and candidates, helped to fuel the suspicion that any form of third-party spending is vaguely illicit. Many Quebec interest groups specifically mentioned the possibilities for corruption or influence-peddling as compelling reasons to ban it.

Although neither the type of group nor the proportion of group revenue derived from government sources had a significant impact on attitudes toward third-party spending, the variations found in tables 2.13 and 2.14 are nonetheless suggestive. As far as the type of group is concerned, organizations that might be considered "oppositional," or critical of the status quo – labour-agricultural, moral-ethical and environmental – are the only ones in favour of third-party spending. A majority of business groups (53.8 percent), social service groups (69.8 percent) and noneconomic interests (66.7 percent) are opposed to this practice. Groups that receive no government funding are most supportive of unrestricted third-party spending, as table 2.14 demonstrates. There is

Table 2.14
Attitudes toward third-party spending, by government revenue

Should groups be allowed to spend?	Government revenue (%)		
	None	1–50%	> 50%
No	41.7	92.9	57.4
Yes	58.3	7.1	42.6

Kendall's tau-c = -.06; p = .28.

Table 2.15
Attitudes toward third-party spending, by satisfaction with MP

Should groups be allowed to spend?	Satisfaction (%)		
	Not satisfied	Somewhat satisfied	Very satisfied
No	42.1	47.6	68.3
Yes	57.9	52.4	31.7

Kendall's tau-c = -.25; p < .05.

a curious curvilinear relationship between government revenue and attitudes toward third-party spending: organizations that receive less than half of their annual budget from government are almost unanimously opposed to the practice of interest group election spending; those receiving more than 50 percent of their revenues from government are about equally divided on the issue. These data should not be overemphasized since the relationship is an exceedingly weak one, but table 2.14 seems to suggest that groups that actively seek government financing, but whose state funding remains precarious, are those most likely to want to avoid any hint of partisan activity.

As tables 2.15, 2.16 and 2.17 suggest, the level of group satisfaction with the local MP and the political system in general, as well as the group's assessment of how it fares vis-à-vis other local interest groups in its interactions with its MP, have a strong impact on attitudes toward third-party spending (Kendall's tau-c of –.25, –.24, and –.26 respectively). Those groups dissatisfied with the local MP and the political system as a whole, and which feel that their MP responds to the concerns of other groups more readily than to their own, are most likely to favour relatively unrestricted third-party spending. A strong majority of groups (between 68 percent and 73 percent) that are satisfied with their MP and the

Table 2.16
Attitudes toward third-party spending, by satisfaction with the system

	Satisfaction (%)		
Should groups be allowed to spend?	Not satisfied	Somewhat satisfied	Very satisfied
No	45.9	69.4	71.4
Yes	54.1	30.6	28.6

Kendall's tau-c = -.24; $p < .05$.

Table 2.17
Attitudes toward third-party spending, by MP rank

	Group does ... with MP than other groups (%)		
Should groups be allowed to spend?	Worse	No difference	Better
No	35.3	55.0	73.3
Yes	64.7	45.0	26.7

Kendall's tau-c = -.26; $p < .05$.

political system, and feel that the local MP accords them preferential treatment, are in favour of a ban on interest group election spending.

Finally, table 2.16 confirms the trend noted above: organizations that perceive the political system to favour certain powerful groups are much more likely to favour third-party spending than groups that feel the system is more or less equitable (53.1 to 23.5 percent). Tables 2.15 through 2.18 suggest, then, that interest group election spending is seen by organizations unhappy with the existing political system as a tool for offsetting the power of entrenched vested interests. Indeed, comments gleaned from the interviews indicate that this sort of spending constitutes one of the few methods whereby groups that feel they are shut out of the system can make their concerns known to politicians and the public. Thus, even if a majority of interest groups feel that third-party spending during elections ought to be banned because the practice favours more affluent groups or is open to corruption, a total prohibition on this activity would likely only add to the sense of frustration felt by those organizations most dissatisfied with the present political system.

On the broader question of reforming the political system to make it more responsive to the needs and demands of local interest groups, less than half the organizations interviewed were able to put forward

Table 2.18
Attitudes toward third-party spending, by perception of unequal group power

| | Are there groups that are too powerful? (%) | |
Should groups be allowed to spend?	No	Yes
No	76.5	46.9
Yes	23.5	53.1

Kendall's tau-b = .30; p < .01.

Table 2.19
Attitudes toward reform with group budget

| | Budget (%) | | |
Type of reform	$100 000 & under	$100 000 – 999 999	More than $1 million
Consult-decentralize	20.8	41.7	60.0
Political	79.2	58.2	40.0

Kendall's tau-c = -.31; p < .05.

specific proposals for change, as opposed to vague calls for improved consultation. Thirty-one groups (almost 35 percent of the sample) declined to answer this question, either because they had no idea of the kind of reforms necessary or, as was usually the case, because they were relatively happy with the existing system. Of the remaining groups, the most common response (mentioned by 14 groups, almost 15 percent of the total sample) was to call for "greater consultation" or "*real* consultation" (as opposed to the charade in which many groups felt the government was engaged). Another seven groups (8 percent of the total sample) urged the government to decentralize its operations and allow community organizations a more active role in the decision-making process. Thirty-seven groups (just under 47 percent of the total sample) did propose specific political or organizational reforms to make the system more responsive. Many of these proposals centred on the need to make the local MP more accountable to constituents, possibly by relaxing the strict party discipline characteristic of British-style parliamentary government. As the spokesman for one environmental organization put it, there is a need to "take the whip from the party whip and strangle him with it." Seven groups advocated changes in our electoral system to give a greater voice to local interest groups, either through more frequent use of referendums or through the implementation of a system

Table 2.20
Attitudes toward reform with satisfaction with MP

Type of reform	Level of satisfaction (%)		
	Not satisfied	Somewhat satisfied	Very satisfied
Consult-decentralize	6.7	40.0	48.1
Political	93.3	60.0	51.9

Kendall's tau-c = -.34; $p < .01$.

Table 2.21
Attitudes toward reform with special election strategy

Type of reform	Special strategy (%)	
	No	Yes
Consult-decentralize	44.4	8.3
Political	55.6	91.7

Kendall's tau-b = .31; $p < .05$.

of proportional representation. Finally, some organizations called for general reforms of the bureaucracy, to reduce red tape and to lessen the power of individual bureaucrats.

Several variables affected a group's attitudes toward reform. Groups with relatively small budgets were more likely to call for political reforms, as opposed to vague recommendations for greater consultation or decentralization, than were their wealthier counterparts (table 2.19). A desire for specific political reforms was also related to a group's satisfaction with its MP. The more dissatisfied the group, the more in favour of political change it was likely to be (table 2.20). Not surprisingly, groups advocating political change were most likely to pursue special media and contacting strategies during an election campaign (table 2.21). All of this tends to confirm our earlier finding that a group's perception of the fairness of the political system has a marked impact on its contacting strategies (the type of interaction it has with politicians, the media and the political system in general) and on its desire for political reform, including its willingness to allow third-party spending during election campaigns.

MPs' EVALUATIONS OF THE SYSTEM

As was mentioned earlier, the limited number of interviews conducted with members of Parliament prevented us from making solid generalizations about their assessment of the role of local interest groups in the political process. Several observations can nonetheless be drawn from our extremely limited sample of MPs. Most of the MPs indicated that dealing with interest groups occupied at most 25 percent of their working day. Some reported that handling individual inquiries from constituents – especially those regarding immigration – was far more demanding than dealing with interest groups. Virtually all of the MPs interviewed (six of seven) claimed that the lobbying techniques of interest groups had become markedly more sophisticated in recent years, but only one was willing to admit that it was increasingly difficult for the local member of Parliament to cope with these pressure tactics. One MP noted that a great deal of staff time was required to respond to some of the better organized groups. He also said that some groups clearly have unrealistic expectations about MPs' accessibility or their ability to respond to every single interest group inquiry. He gave the example of a campaign by local music teachers to protest against the GST. They encouraged their students to mail form letters to the constituency office for an exemption from the tax. Veterinary clinics, bookstores and libraries undertook similar campaigns, with the result that it was impossible for the MP to respond to all the material crossing his desk.

Despite the growing sophistication of interest group tactics, and their frequently unrealistic expectations of the local MP and the political system, almost all the MPs interviewed felt that the groups' interventions in the political process – to promote a candidate or cause, or target political parties or their standard-bearers – were effective and beneficial. Interest group activities of this nature, said one MP, provide local politicians with much needed information on crucial issues and provoke debate. Another, although also noting that interest group intervention in elections served a vital communications function, worried that many of the most active groups represented "extreme" viewpoints. Only three MPs acknowledged that they had been negatively targeted by an interest group; in all three cases pro-life organizations had singled them out.

Most MPs agreed that the media and interest groups manipulate each other to sensationalize issues. According to one MP, a new "subculture" was emerging in his riding, which he labelled the "professional demonstrator." These activist elements, he claimed, often undermined the effectiveness of the larger organization to which they nominally belonged. Another MP, perhaps optimistically, argued that groups trying to engage in this media-centred style of politics often ended up "getting burned" or fizzling out, and thus there was no compelling reason to get worked up about this phenomenon. Indeed, most MPs seemed resigned to dealing with an aggressive, and at times manipulative, media. It is in the nature of the modern mass media to focus on controversy, provide good visuals and simplify complex issues (however absurdly). At best, the MPs argued, we can hope for more objective reporting from the fourth and fifth estates.

Finally, on the question of third-party election spending, five of the seven MPs were unwilling to support an outright ban, principally because such spending was seen as part of the democratic process or as fundamental to freedom of speech. Some MPs nonetheless worried about the prospect of elected officials becoming beholden to groups that bankrolled their campaigns, as appears to have happened in the United States. Two MPs advocated ceilings on third-party spending, therefore, to preserve a modicum of equity in the system. In this respect, the MPs' views paralleled those of the 40 percent or so of interest groups in favour of some sort of regulation of third-party spending, short of imposing a complete ban on the activity.

CONCLUSION

The portrait of the political activity of local interest groups that emerges from the preceding analysis is considerably at odds with the popular view in the media that these organizations exert an exaggerated influence on contemporary politics. None of the local members of Parliament interviewed – although the number was admittedly small – endorsed this notion. They tended to argue that interest groups, even those with offensive tactics or unrealistic demands, served an important communications function in the political system and sparked much-needed debate on issues of public policy.

As for the groups themselves, most tend to be dissatisfied with the political system in general, although quite favourably disposed to their local MPs. This dissatisfaction appears to be one of the key variables explaining the level of group activity and the perceived need for reform of the political system. Those groups that felt the political system and the federal government were unresponsive to their concerns were most likely to favour relatively unrestricted spending by interest groups during election campaigns as one of the few means at their disposal to make their concerns heard. Thus, despite the widespread belief that wealthy groups, especially those representing business interests, stand to benefit the most from unregulated third-party spending, at the local level these are precisely the groups most likely to favour a ban on this activity. It is oppositional groups, those unhappy with the existing system or critical of the established political order, that are most likely to favour relatively unrestrained third-party spending during elections. This finding should give pause to those reformers who seek to ban third-party spending outright, in the name of greater electoral equity.

APPENDIX A
LIST OF INTEREST GROUPS INTERVIEWED

AIDS Network of Edmonton
Alliance for the Preservation of English Canada
Amitié Soleil
Architectural Clearing House Association
Atelier ensemble on s'tient
Big Sisters Association of Saskatoon
Bissell Community Centre
Boyle Street Co-op
Brockville and Area Pro-Choice Committee
Brockville Area Community Living Association
Brockville Right to Life
Budd Canada
Cadillac Wheat Pool Committee
Campaign Life Coalition – Kingston
Canadian Abortion Rights Action League – Kingston
Catholic Social Services
Cegep Lionel-Groulx
Centre des Femmes de Montréal
Chatham Outreach for Hunger
Chatham-Kent Small Business Support Corporation
Chatham-Kent Women's Centre Inc.
Citizens Against Sexual Child Abuse
CLSC St-Henri
CLSC Metro
Club de l'âge d'or de Saint-Eustache
Commission Industrielle de Mirabel Sud
Communities for Controlled Prostitution
Council on Aging
Edmonton and District Labour Council
Edmonton Association of Engineers
Edmonton Immigrant Services Association
Elizabeth Fry Society
Family Focus of Leeds and Grenville
Family Services
Friends of Rondeau Park
Global Community Centre
Kingston and Area Economic Development Commission
Kingston and District Immigration Services
Kingston and District Labour Council
Kingston Environmental Action Project
Kingston Interval House
Kingston Lesbian and Gay Association
Lakeshore Vocational Project Association Inc.

Leeds and Grenville Children's Services Advisory Group
Les Grands Frères et Les Grandes Sœurs de L'Ouest de L'Île
Limestone Advisory Centre for Community Projects
McCauley Health Centre
Mennonite Centre for Newcomers
Montreal Children's Hospital
Napanee Region Conservation Authority
National Association of English Rights
Native Friendship Centre of Montreal, Inc.
North Hastings Business Development Centre
Odessa Agricultural Society
Ontario Alliance for English Rights – Brockville
Operation Friendship
Operation Our Kids
Paper Chase Recycling
People in Need of Shelter Society
People Working and Learning Manufacturing Inc.
Perspective communautaire en santé mentale
Project Ploughshares
Refugee Action Committee
Reid, Crowther, and Partners
Right to Life, Kent
Sandhills Community Development Project
Sandhills Housing Cooperative
Saskatoon and District Labour Council
Saskatoon and District Tribal Council
Saskatoon Board of Trade
Saskatoon Branch – Association for Community Living
Saskatoon Multicultural Council
Saskatoon Open Door Society
Service d'aide aux néo-québécois et aux immigrants Inc. (Sanqui)
Société de développement économique de Groulx
Société d'initiative et de développement d'artères commerciales
Space Science Centre
Teen Aid Saskatoon
The Mutual Group
Transport 2000
Tyendinaga Indian Reserve
Ukrainian Canadian Social Services
Waterloo Chamber of Commerce
Waterloo Regional Labour Council
Waterloo Right to Life
West Island Business Development Council
West Island Citizen Advocacy
World Food Day Committee
Youth Horizons

APPENDIX B
INTEREST GROUP INTERVIEW

Name of interviewer: _____

Name of person being interviewed: _____

Position of person being interviewed: _____

Date and place of interview: _____

A. INTEREST GROUP STRUCTURE

1. How long has your group been in existence? _____

2. What are the goals of your organization? (Probe for the degree of issue-oriented activity.)_____

3. What is your group's budget (approximate)? _____

4. Approximately what proportion of your group's revenue comes from government sources?

   ❏ Over 50%   ❏ 25–50%   ❏ Under 25%   ❏ None

5. What is the size of your group's membership? _____

6. What is the size of your group's full-time paid staff? _____

7. What is the size of your group's part-time paid staff? _____

8. What is the size of your group's voluntary staff? _____

9. Do other local groups provide services similar to yours?

   ❏ Yes   ❏ No

   If yes, specify _____

10. Do you regularly work with any of these groups?

    ❏ Yes   ❏ No

    If yes, elaborate _____

B. CONTACTS WITH POLITICIANS

11. Approximately how often have you contacted your sitting MP since the federal election of November 21, 1988? _____

12. What was the nature of these contacts? _____

13. How satisfied have you been with your federal MP's (insert name) response? _____

    ❏ Very satisfied   ❏ Somewhat satisfied   ❏ Not satisfied

14. What kinds of contact have you had with your MPP/MLA/MNA (insert name)?_____

15. How satisfied have you been with your MPP's response?

    ❐ Very satisfied   ❐ Somewhat satisfied   ❐ Not satisfied

16. What kinds of contact have you had with your local political representatives?_____

17. How satisfied have you been with your local political representatives' response?

    ❐ Very satisfied   ❐ Somewhat satisfied   ❐ Not satisfied

18. Did you contact the federal Conservative candidate during the 1988 election campaign?

    ❐ Yes   ❐ No

19. Did you provide any support for the Conservative candidate during the 1988 election campaign?

    ❐ Yes   ❐ No

    If yes, elaborate _____

20. Did you contact the federal Liberal candidate during the 1988 election campaign?

    ❐ Yes   ❐ No

21. Did you provide any support for the Liberal candidate during the 1988 election campaign?

    ❐ Yes   ❐ No

    If yes, elaborate _____

22. Did you contact the federal NDP candidate during the 1988 election campaign?

    ❐ Yes   ❐ No

23. Did you provide any support for the NDP candidate during the 1988 election campaign?

    ❐ Yes   ❐ No

    If yes, elaborate _____

24. Did you contact the candidate for any other federal political party during the 1988 election campaign?

    ❐ Yes   ❐ No

    If yes, specify _____

25. Did you provide any support for this candidate during the 1988 election campaign?

    ❐ Yes   ❐ No

    If yes, elaborate _____

26. Has your MP ever initiated a contact with your group?

    ❏ Yes   ❏ No

    If yes, what was the nature of the contact(s)?_____

C. PUBLIC RELATIONS

27. Do you see it as part of your group's objectives to communicate with the public about your goals?

    ❏ Yes   ❏ No

28. If yes, how do you accomplish this?_____

29. Do you pursue this objective differently during federal election campaigns?

    ❏ Yes   ❏ No

    If yes, elaborate _____

30. How frequently do you contact the local media?

    _____

31. How satisfied are you with coverage by the media?

    ❏ Very satisfied   ❏ Somewhat satisfied   ❏ Not satisfied

32. Do you feel that your group's message is reaching the public effectively?

    ❏ Yes   ❏ No

    If no, elaborate _____

33. How satisfied are you with the public's response to your group's message?

    ❏ Very satisfied   ❏ Somewhat satisfied   ❏ Not satisfied

D. EVALUATION OF SYSTEM

34. How satisfied are you with the way the political system in general responds to your group?

    ❏ Very satisfied   ❏ Somewhat satisfied   ❏ Not satisfied

    ❏ Not applicable

35. How satisfied are you with the way the federal Conservative government responds to your group?

    ❏ Very satisfied   ❏ Somewhat satisfied   ❏ Not satisfied

    ❏ Not applicable

36. How satisfied are you with the way the federal Liberal party responds to your group?

  ❑ Very satisfied   ❑ Somewhat satisfied   ❑ Not satisfied

  ❑ Not applicable

37. How satisfied are you with the way the federal NDP party responds to your group?

  ❑ Very satisfied   ❑ Somewhat satisfied   ❑ Not satisfied

  ❑ Not applicable

38. How satisfied are you with the way the provincial Conservative party responds to your group?

  ❑ Very satisfied   ❑ Somewhat satisfied   ❑ Not satisfied

  ❑ Not applicable

39. How satisfied are you with the way the provincial Liberal party responds to your group?

  ❑ Very satisfied   ❑ Somewhat satisfied   ❑ Not satisfied

  ❑ Not applicable

40. How satisfied are you with the way the provincial NDP responds to your group?

  ❑ Very satisfied   ❑ Somewhat satisfied   ❑ Not satisfied

  ❑ Not applicable

41. How satisfied are you with the way the local government responds to your group?

  ❑ Very satisfied   ❑ Somewhat satisfied   ❑ Not satisfied

  ❑ Not applicable

42. How well do you think your local MP responds to your group's concerns in comparison with other groups' concerns?

  ❑ Your group does better in comparison.

  ❑ Your group does no differently in comparison.

  ❑ Your group does worse in comparison.

43. How well do you think the federal Conservative government responds to your group's concerns in comparison with other groups' concerns?

  ❑ Your group does better in comparison.

  ❑ Your group does no differently in comparison.

  ❑ Your group does worse in comparison.

44. How well do you think the federal Liberal party responds to your group's concerns in comparison with other groups' concerns?

   ❏ Your group does better in comparison.

   ❏ Your group does no differently in comparison.

   ❏ Your group does worse in comparison.

45. How well do you think the federal NDP responds to your group's concerns in comparison with other groups' concerns?

   ❏ Your group does better in comparison.

   ❏ Your group does no differently in comparison.

   ❏ Your group does worse in comparison.

46. How well do you think the provincial government responds to your group's concerns in comparison with other groups' concerns?

   ❏ Your group does better in comparison.

   ❏ Your group does no differently in comparison.

   ❏ Your group does worse in comparison.

47. How well do you think the local government responds to your group's concerns in comparison with other groups' concerns?

   ❏ Your group does better in comparison.

   ❏ Your group does no differently in comparison.

   ❏ Your group does worse in comparison.

48. Do you think that there are any other local groups that have too much influence in the political process?

   ❏ Yes   ❏ No

   If yes, elaborate _____

49. Do you think local interest groups should be able to spend money on and provide other resources for candidates and parties that favour their cause?

   ❏ Yes   ❏ No

   Please give reasons for your answer _____

50. If you could make suggestions to allow the political system to be more responsive to local groups like yours, what would they be?

   _____

   _____

APPENDIX C
SURVEY OF PARTISAN ÉLITES

Name of interviewer: _____

Name of person being interviewed: _____

Position of person being interviewed: _____

Date and place of interview: _____

1. On the average, approximately what proportion of your working day is spent dealing with interest groups?

   ❑ Less than 10%   ❑ 10–25%   ❑ 25–50%   ❑ More than 50%

2. What are the main kinds of interest groups that contact you?

   _____

3. On the whole, are the groups most likely to contact you those that have relatively large memberships or those with smaller memberships?

   ❑ Large memberships   ❑ Small memberships   ❑ Both equally

   ❑ Not applicable   ❑ Don't know

4. Do groups with large memberships interact with you differently than those with small memberships?

   ❑ Yes   ❑ No

   If yes, elaborate _____

5. Do groups with single-issue goals interact with you differently than those with more general objectives?

   ❑ Yes   ❑ No

   If yes, elaborate _____

6. On the whole, are the groups most likely to contact you those with purely local concerns or are they branches of national interest groups?

   ❑ Local   ❑ National   ❑ Both equally

   ❑ Not applicable   ❑ Don't know

7. On the whole, do groups with local concerns interact with you differently than those with national objectives?

   ❑ Yes   ❑ No

   If yes, elaborate _____

8. Do you feel that the lobbying techniques of interest groups have become more sophisticated over time, less sophisticated or have they stayed about the same?

   ❏ More   ❏ Less   ❏ About the same

   If less, elaborate _____

9. Is it increasingly difficult for MPs to deal with these lobbying techniques?

   ❏ Yes   ❏ No

   If yes, elaborate _____

10. Do you find that groups are more or less likely to contact you during election campaigns compared with other times?

    ❏ More likely   ❏ Less likely

    If less likely, elaborate _____

11. Are interest groups an excessive drain on your working time?

    ❏ Yes   ❏ No

    If yes, elaborate _____

12. Have you ever been negatively targeted by interest groups?

    ❏ Yes   ❏ No

    If yes, elaborate _____

13. Have you ever been assisted in elections by interest groups?

    ❏ Yes   ❏ No

    If yes, elaborate _____

14. Do you believe that, generally speaking, the targeting campaigns of interest groups are effective or ineffective?

    ❏ Effective   ❏ Ineffective

    Please give reasons for your answer _____

15. Do you believe that the targeting campaigns of interest groups are good for the political process?

    ❏ Yes   ❏ No

    Why? _____

16. Do you think that local interest groups should be able to spend money and provide other resources for candidates and parties that favour their cause?

    ❏ Yes   ❏ No

    Please give reasons for your answer _____

17. How much impact on the vote do you feel that local interest groups have (that is, how many votes are their activities likely to sway)?

Express as an approximate percentage of voters in the constituency ____

18. Are there ever instances when you want to assist in the interest group's objectives being communicated to the public?

❒ Yes   ❒ No

If yes, elaborate _____

19. Are there ever any occasions when you initiate contact with a local interest group?

❒ Yes   ❒ No

If yes, please indicate why, and give specific examples _____

20. Do you have any reservations about the way the media cover interest groups' activity?

❒ Yes   ❒ No

If yes, elaborate _____

21. Do you feel that the messages of local interest groups are reaching the public effectively?

❒ Yes   ❒ No

If yes, elaborate _____

22. Do interest groups and the media use each other to unduly dramatize issues?

❒ Yes   ❒ No

If yes, elaborate _____

23. Are there changes in the system that you would like to see?

_____

NOTES

We would like to thank Ruth Thomson, Alain Desruisseaux, Christine Campbell, Brian Humphreys, Sylvain Côté and Peter Bergbusch for their research assistance. We are also grateful to the interest group representatives and the members of Parliament who consented to be interviewed for this study.

1. Maude Barlow, one of the founding members of the Pro-Canada Network, the principal anti-free trade organization, remarked that pro-free trade forces "outspent us four or five times. Big business bought this election" (quoted in Gray 1989, 17). Hiebert (1991, table 1) estimates that the Canadian Alliance for Trade and Job Opportunities, the influential business lobby that

campaigned vigorously for free trade during the 1988 election, spent approximately $2.3 million on its campaign. By contrast, the Pro-Canada Network spent just under $800 000 during the election.

2. There have been virtually no restrictions on third-party spending at the federal level since the decision of the Alberta Supreme Court in 1984 to strike down amendments to section 70.1 of the *Canada Elections Act* (contained in Bill C-169, passed one year earlier). The 1983 amendments removed the "good faith" defence for organizations or individuals who incurred election expenses (see Seidle 1985, 125).

3. This attempt had to be abandoned in the face of the total unwillingness of Nova Scotian MPs to cooperate with our research. A number of them made the analogy between the relations of an MP with local interest groups and lawyer-client relations, and to put it colloquially, told us we ought to butt out. Although this analogy seemed absurd, it was futile to press the matter.

4. Given the small number of labour and agricultural groups selected for the study, we were forced to combine these two categories for statistical analysis.

5. Of the six groups falling into the environmental-consumer category, five are purely environmental organizations. The sixth, Transport 2000, described its objectives in terms of consumer advocacy and protection of the environment.

BIBLIOGRAPHY

Canada. Elections Canada. 1988. *Report of the Chief Electoral Officer, Thirty-Fourth General Election*. Ottawa: Minister of Supply and Services Canada.

Fenno, Richard R. 1990. "If, As Ralph Nader Says, Congress is 'The Broken Branch', How Come We Love Our Congressmen So Much?" In *American Government: Readings and Cases*. 10th ed., ed. Peter Woll. Toronto: Little, Brown.

Gray, Charlotte. 1989. "Purchasing Power." *Saturday Night*, March, 15–18.

Hiebert, Janet. 1989–90. "Fair Elections and Freedom of Expression under the Charter." *Journal of Canadian Studies* 24 (Winter): 72–86.

———. 1991. "Interest Groups and Canadian Federal Elections." In *Interest Groups and Elections in Canada*, ed. F. Leslie Seidle. Vol. 2 of the research studies of the Royal Commission on Electoral Reform and Party Financing. Ottawa and Toronto: RCERPF/Dundurn.

Kay, Barry, S. Lambert, S. Brown and J. Curtis. 1989. "Single-Issue Interest Groups and the Canadian Electorate: The Case of Abortion in 1988." Paper presented at the Annual Meeting of the Canadian Political Science Association, Quebec City.

Offe, Claus. 1987. "Challenging the Boundaries of Institutional Politics: Social Movements Since the 1960s." In *Changing Boundaries of the Political,* ed. C.S. Maier. Cambridge: Cambridge University Press.

Paltiel, Khayyam Zev. 1987. "Canadian Election Expense Legislation 1963–85: A Critical Appraisal or Was the Effort Worth It?" In *Contemporary Canadian Politics: Readings and Notes,* ed. R.J. Jackson, D. Jackson and N. Baxter-Moore. Scarborough: Prentice-Hall.

Pross, Paul. 1986. *Group Politics and Public Policy.* Oxford: Oxford University Press.

Public Affairs International. 1990. *The PAI Report.* Toronto.

Seidle, F. Leslie. 1985. "The Election Expenses Act: The House of Commons and the Parties." In *The Canadian House of Commons,* ed. John C. Courtney. Calgary: University of Calgary Press.

CONTRIBUTORS TO VOLUME 2

Janet Hiebert   Commission Research Coordinator
Barry J. Kay   Wilfrid Laurier University
A. Brian Tanguay   Wilfrid Laurier University

ACKNOWLEDGEMENTS

The Royal Commission on Electoral Reform and Party Financing and the publishers wish to acknowledge with gratitude the permission of the following publishers and individuals to reprint and translate material from their works:

David Adamany, Wayne State University; *Arizona Law Review*; McGill-Queen's University Press; Minister of Supply and Services Canada.

Care has been taken to trace the ownership of copyright material used in the text, including the tables and figures. The authors and publishers welcome any information enabling them to rectify any reference or credit in subsequent editions.

Consistent with the Commission's objective of promoting full participation in the electoral system by all segments of Canadian society, gender neutrality has been used wherever possible in the editing of the research studies.

THE COLLECTED RESEARCH STUDIES*

---

* The titles of studies may not be final in all cases.

ROBERT E. MUTCH — The Evolution of Campaign Finance Regulation in the United States and Canada

JANE JENSON — Innovation and Equity: The Impact of Public Funding

MICHAEL PINTO-DUSCHINSKY — The Party Foundations and Political Finance in Germany

VOLUME 5
Issues in Party and Election Finance in Canada
F. Leslie Seidle, Editor

LISA YOUNG — Toward Transparency: An Evaluation of Disclosure Arrangements in Canadian Political Finance

MICHAEL KRASHINSKY AND WILLIAM J. MILNE — Some Evidence on the Effects of Incumbency in the 1988 Canadian Federal Election

R. KENNETH CARTY — Official Agents in Canadian Elections: The Case of the 1988 General Election

D. KEITH HEINTZMAN — Electoral Competition, Campaign Expenditure and Incumbency Advantage

THOMAS S. AXWORTHY — Capital-Intensive Politics: Money, Media and Mores in the United States and Canada

PETER P. CONSTANTINOU — Public Funding of Political Parties, Candidates and Elections in Canada

ERIC BERTRAM — Independent Candidates in Federal General Elections

DONALD PADGET — Large Contributions to Candidates in the 1988 Federal Election and the Issue of Undue Influence

PASCALE MICHAUD AND PIERRE LAFERRIÈRE — Economic Analysis of the Funding of Political Parties in Canada

VOLUME 6
Women in Canadian Politics: Toward Equity in Representation
Kathy Megyery, Editor

JANINE BRODIE, WITH THE ASSISTANCE OF CELIA CHANDLER — Women and the Electoral Process in Canada

VOLUME 9

Aboriginal Peoples and Electoral Reform in Canada
Robert A. Milen, Editor

ROBERT A. MILEN	Aboriginal Constitutional and Electoral Reform
AUGIE FLERAS	Aboriginal Electoral Districts for Canada: Lessons from New Zealand
VALERIE ALIA	Aboriginal Peoples and Campaign Coverage in the North
ROGER GIBBINS	Electoral Reform and Canada's Aboriginal Population: An Assessment of Aboriginal Electoral Districts

VOLUME 10

Democratic Rights and Electoral Reform in Canada
Michael Cassidy, Editor

JENNIFER SMITH	The Franchise and Theories of Representative Government
PIERRE LANDREVILLE AND LUCIE LEMONDE	Voting Rights for Inmates
YVES DENONCOURT	Reflections concerning Criteria for the Vote for Persons with Mental Disorders
PATRICE GARANT	Political Rights of Public Servants in the Political Process
KENNETH KERNAGHAN	The Political Rights of Canada's Federal Public Servants
PETER MCCORMICK	Provision for the Recall of Elected Officials: Parameters and Prospects
DAVID MAC DONALD	Referendums and Federal General Elections
JOHN C. COURTNEY AND DAVID E. SMITH	Registering Voters: Canada in a Comparative Context
CÉCILE BOUCHER	Administration and Enforcement of the Elections Act in Canada

VOLUME 13

Canadian Political Parties: Leaders, Candidates and Organization
Herman Bakvis, Editor

VOLUME 14

Representation, Integration and Political Parties in Canada
Herman Bakvis, Editor

VOLUME 23
Canadian Political Parties in the Constituencies: A Local Perspective

R. KENNETH CARTY   Canadian Political Parties in the
                                    Constituencies: A Local Perspective

COMMISSION ORGANIZATION

CHAIRMAN
Pierre Lortie

COMMISSIONERS
Pierre Fortier
Robert Gabor
William Knight
Lucie Pépin

SENIOR OFFICERS

Executive Director
Guy Goulard

Director of Research
Peter Aucoin

Special Adviser to the Chairman
Jean-Marc Hamel

Research
F. Leslie Seidle,
  Senior Research Coordinator

Legislation
Jules Brière, Senior Adviser
Gérard Bertrand
Patrick Orr

Coordinators
Herman Bakvis
Michael Cassidy
Frederick J. Fletcher
Janet Hiebert
Kathy Megyery
Robert A. Milen
David Small

Communications and Publishing
Richard Rochefort, Director
Hélène Papineau, Assistant
  Director
Paul Morisset, Editor
Kathryn Randle, Editor

Assistant Coordinators
David Mac Donald
Cheryl D. Mitchell

Finance and Administration
Maurice R. Lacasse, Director

Contracts and Personnel
Thérèse Lacasse, Chief

EDITORIAL, DESIGN AND PRODUCTION SERVICES

ROYAL COMMISSION ON ELECTORAL REFORM AND PARTY FINANCING

Editors   Denis Bastien, Susan Becker Davidson, Ginette Bertrand, Louis Bilodeau, Claude Brabant, Louis Chabot, Danielle Chaput, Norman Dahl, Carlos del Burgo, Julie Desgagners, Chantal Granger, Volker Junginger, Denis Landry, André LaRose, Paul Morisset, Christine O'Meara, Mario Pelletier, Marie-Noël Pichelin, Kathryn Randle, Georges Royer, Eve Valiquette, Dominique Vincent.

LE CENTRE DE DOCUMENTATION JURIDIQUE DU QUÉBEC INC.

Hubert Reid, *President*

Claire Grégoire, *Comptroller*

Lucie Poirier, *Production Manager*
Gisèle Gingras, *Special Project Assistant*

Translators   Pierre-Yves de la Garde, Richard Lapointe, Marie-Josée Turcotte.

Technical Editors   Stéphane Côté Coulombe, *Coordinator;*
Josée Chabot, Danielle Morin.

Copy Editors   Martine Germain, Lise Larochelle, Elisabeth Reid, Carole St-Louis, Isabelle Tousignant, Charles Tremblay, Sébastien Viau.

Word Processing   André Vallée.

Formatting   Typoform, Claude Audet; Linda Goudreau, *Formatting Coordinator.*

WILSON & LAFLEUR LTÉE

Claude Wilson, *President*

Printed in Canada